Mahatma Gandhi

The Most Famous Political Activist of India

(How One Passionate Peacemaker Gently Shook the World)

Julius Wells

Published By **Darby Connor**

Julius Wells

All Rights Reserved

Mahatma Gandhi: The Most Famous Political Activist of India (How One Passionate Peacemaker Gently Shook the World)

ISBN 978-1-77485-726-7

No part of this guidebook shall be reproduced in any form without permission in writing from the publisher except in the case of brief quotations embodied in critical articles or reviews.

Legal & Disclaimer

The information contained in this ebook is not designed to replace or take the place of any form of medicine or professional medical advice. The information in this ebook has been provided for educational & entertainment purposes only.

The information contained in this book has been compiled from sources deemed reliable, and it is accurate to the best of the Author's knowledge; however, the Author cannot guarantee its accuracy and validity and cannot be held liable for any errors or omissions. Changes are periodically made to this book. You must consult your doctor or get professional medical advice before using any of the suggested remedies, techniques, or information in this book.

Upon using the information contained in this book, you agree to hold harmless the Author from and against any damages, costs, and expenses, including any legal fees potentially resulting from the application of any of the information provided by this guide. This disclaimer applies to any damages or injury caused by the use and application, whether directly or indirectly, of any advice or information presented, whether for breach of contract, tort, negligence, personal injury, criminal intent, or under any other cause of action.

You agree to accept all risks of using the information presented inside this book. You need to consult a professional medical practitioner in order to ensure you are both able and healthy enough to participate in this program.

Table Of Contents

Chapter 1: The Early Life Of Mahatma Gandhi _____ 1

Chapter 2: Gandhi In South Africa _____ 18

Chapter 3: Gandhi And The Indian Independence Movement _____ 42

Chapter 4: Of Gandhi's End Years _____ 72

Chapter 5: Gandhi's Practiques And Beliefs _____ 79

Chapter 6: Mahatma Gandhi's Legacy Mahatma Gandhi _____ 92

Chapter 7: Who Was Mahatma Gandhi? 95

Chapter 8: What Was The Reason The Mahatma His Name? Mahatma? _____ 152

Chapter 1: The Early Life Of Mahatma Gandhi

"Ours is a constant fight against the degradation that we want to be inflicted by the Europeans who wish to reduce us to the same level as the bare Kaffir who's occupation is hunting and whose primary goal is to gather a certain amount of cattle that he can buy an heir and later, live his existence in nakedness and indolence." -- Gandhi in his address in 1896.

An extensive study of the life and backgrounds of world-renowned leaders frequently sheds light on the way in which they gained their fame as is the case for Mahatma Gandhi. His childhood, experiences, and his upbringing played an important part in shaping his beliefs and practices in the future. According to Gandhi himself wrote, "A variety of incidents that have occurred in my life have brought me into close proximity to people of diverse faiths and communities. My experience with them all supports the claim that I have made no distinction between my relatives and strangers, countrymen or foreigners, colored and white, Hindus and Indians of other religions, whether Muslims, Parsis, Christians or Jews. I can claim that my heart was not able to make such distinctions."[11

Mohandas Karamchand Gandhi was born on the 2nd of October, 1869 in the coastal city of Porbandar which is one of the many tiny states that are currently located in Gujarat. In his autobiography, "Gandhis come from the Bania caste and appear to have been the first farmers," which is apt since the name Gandhi is a reference to "grocer."[3But Gandhi's father and grandfather were grocers; they were both politicians, who as per Gandhi were faithful to their states. It is worth noting that only 12 years prior to Gandhi's birth in 1857, the uprising was the catalyst for the establishment of the British Raj which was the name given to the state of Porbandar. of Porbandar was among dozens of Indian states run by an Indian prince who was overseen by an official known as a British Resident, who was the real ruler. The modern India was governed by the British Raj contained more than 500 states that had power structures also included an Indian prince, who was under the aegis of an British representative. [4]

The father of Gandhi, Karamchand Gandhi, was an extremely faithful civil servant, since he was the powerful diwan (chief minister) of the Porbandar state. According to Gandhi wrote in the autobiography of his father, the family he was born into belonged to the caste of commercial Banias although this caste was third in the Hindu social hierarchy, after Brahmins and Kshatriyas Banias were generally considered to be the highest caste. The environment Gandhi was brought up in and the stories that he heard about the achievements of his father as well as his great-grandparents, surely affected Gandhi and his thinking. Although his family was not in any way wealthy, per Gandhi, "my father never ever had a desire to become wealth and left us with small assets," what he lacked in terms of money, he made up for with the extensive political experience that his dad had. 6. Gandhi stated about his dad, "He had no education beyond the experience he gained through his life. In the best case, he can be considered to have studied all the way to fifth Gujarati standard. In terms of geography and history, He was uninvolved. However, his extensive knowledge of practical issues put him well in solving the most difficult questions and in the management of hundreds of people. In terms of religious education, he had only a few however, he was able to enjoy the type of religious tradition that frequent trips to temples as well as hearing religious talks make accessible for many Hindus. In his final days, he began to read the Gita on the advice of a knowledgeable Brahman close friend from the family. He often read aloud certain scriptures every day during times of worship."[77

His Mother, Gandhi also wrote extensively. Contrary to his father who was very active in politics of the state however, he was mostly uninterested in the religious sphere, Gandhi's mom was an extremely religious woman who "would not even consider eating her meals in the absence of her regular prayers."[8Putlibai's devotion to God and devotion to God left a lasting influence on Gandhi who was a child watching her pray fervently in temples, observe up to 3 consecutive days of fasting, and fulfill her daily religious obligations even when sick. It was through the mother of his father that Gandhi realized the importance of a strict diet and adhering to a religious belief.

Images of Gandhi's parents

Gandhi was raised in a very diverse religious setting. In addition to the long-lasting impression his mother's piety had in him Gandhi became acquainted with a variety of other religions throughout his life. Many of his parents' friends were Jains who practiced an uncompromising principle of non-violence, humility, and self-control. Gandhi had also been exposed to Christian missionaries, but the first contact with Christianity wasn't as significant of an influence in his early years as it would later in his life when he met Christian friends during his time in London. But the fact that, as a child was he exposed to different opinions - some of which were incompatible, while others were that were not - was the basis of his beliefs about equality and peace in the young Gandhi.

At seven years old, Gandhi left Porbandar and relocated from there to Rajkot along with his dad, who was named a judge of the Rajasthanik Court. Gandhi remembered his time in the primary school very well, highlighting the aspect that he was quite shy, and was a poor student at the very best. However, his school years weren't an influence on his life however. While Gandhi did not like reading, and often avoided studying beyond the school textbooks but he was able to find an old book about the show Shravana Pitribhakti Nataka and it focused on the character Shravana's commitment towards his family. According to Gandhi later wrote, "the book and the photo of Shravana taking his parents who were blind in a journey to the templemade an image in my mind."[10A different play that was awe-inspiring to Gandhi particularly was Harishchandra and is about the legend about a person who stood by his word and never told a lie throughout his life. Gandhi was profoundly inspired by the advantages of being honest as he read the play, and his initial identification with these ideas of devotion, love, and truth as the most important human values can be traced to the stories that shocked him at such a young age. As Gandhi stated in his autobiography "My intuition tells me that Harishchandra would not have been the historical persona. But the two characters Harishchandra and Shravana are real-life characters for me and I'm sure I'd be moved just the same way as I was should I go back and read these plays today."[1111

Gandhi aged 7 years old.

It is fascinating to observe that Gandhi's childhood did not have any significant encounter with imperialism as was prominent within the daily lives of other revolutionaries and resistance leaders in this century. Perhaps due to the fact that his father was an official who was proud to work in the system of political power which was created through his country's British in India His childhood was quite free of the negative narratives of imperialism, colonialism or British government that were typical of the childhoods of many other revolutionaries in the region. It was perhaps because of this lack of animosity and anger from early memories which led to Gandhi was later inspired to study in Britain and then traveled across the ocean to London.

In 1883, after Gandhi turned 13 years old, Gandhi was married to an unnamed girl Kasturbai also thirteen. It was not a wedding however, it was an arranged child marriage, which was arranged by both families. The bitter experience of getting married at an early age caused Gandhi to become an ardent opposition to child marriage later in his life. Gandhi later on recalled that he didn't fully comprehend the meaning behind marriage. To the young man, it was all about "the possibility of nice clothing and drumming, wedding procession, lavish dinners and a woman to have fun with."[12The preparations for marriage were expensive and complicated which resulted in Gandhi being absent for a year from school. According to him "Marriage between Hindus is not an easy thing to do. It is the parents who are bridesmaids as well as the groom often end up in ruin due to the matter. They waste their time and time. The duration of months is dominated by all the getting ready ..."[13[

Gandhi (left) as well as an 1893 classmate.

Gandhi with Kasturbai and Gandhi in 1902

After his wedding with Kasturbai, Gandhi continued his education in high school, though he was delayed by one year. He was an average student, and was not a shining star at school, but not, nor in the field of physical education. He was particularly struggling to master Sanskrit and regretted not making a commitment to learning the language, because lacking the necessary language skills at his disposal, it was "difficult to be interested in our holy books."[14This experience that caused Gandhi to consider in the idea that "every Hindu boy and girl must be proficient in Sanskrit knowledge," and in fact it was his belief that "in every Indian curriculums of higher education, there should be room to teach Hindi, Sanskrit, Persian, Arabic and English."[15]

Gandhi in 1886

Gandhi ultimately passed the matriculation test in 1887. He went to Samaldas College in Bhavanagar, which was less expensive than the other options that he was considering located in the bustling town of Bombay However, when he arrived at Samaldas College, he found himself "entirely in the middle of the ocean. The entire experience was difficult. I was unable to be able to follow, let alone have an interest in professors lecture. This was not the fault of theirs. The faculty members at the College were considered to be top-of-the-line. But I was so naive. When I finished the first semester I went home."[16[16

After this incident, it was that an old friend of the family recommended to Gandhi along with his relatives that Gandhi should be taken to England for studies. The competition for political posts in India was fierce and if Gandhi would like to succeed to his father as diwan of diwan, his family friend suggested that he go to London to be barrister. Upon this, it was explained to him that "he could obtain the diwanship upon asking."[1717

Gandhi was awestruck by the suggestion to quit his studies in the country he was studying even though his mother resisted. Gandhi recorded in his journal of his decision to England and his unwavering determination that "I have said before that I was cowardly. At that point, my cowardice disappeared before the urge to go to England that completely consumed me."[18After pledging in front of his mom that he'd never drink, eat and meat in England His mother granted him the right to study abroad. When he was 1888 Gandhi separated from his spouse and infant and set off to London to learn about law and jurisprudence in The Inner Temple.

In the beginning of his stay during his time in England, Gandhi lived the lifestyle as an English gentleman with a suit for the morning and a top hat carrying a silver-headed chopper. He was taught dance as well as elocution and violin. However, eventually, Gandhi began to realize that these classes and his outfit were not the reason the reason he came to England for. He began to think about some of the more important aspects English life. He began to read widely on British and European laws, politics and economics, as well as interacting with theosophists and scholars, as well as studying religions did not think that he would pursue like Christianity. The newspaper he read and magazines, something he previously not done back in India and he was informed of the current world events by regularly studying such publications like The Daily News, The Telegraph and The Pall Mall Gazette. In this new country, he also read about his own faith and was able to introduce him to the ideas that were the thoughts of Hindu as well as Buddhist philosophers. Gandhi was summoned into the bar on June 1891. He then went to India within two days.

Gandhi as an undergraduate student in London

After returning to India To his complete shock, Gandhi learned that his mother had passed away while she was in London and that his family hidden the news from him in order to avoid the pain of a foreign country. Gandhi was devastated. He later said that "my sorrow was greaterthan that of the death of my father. Many of my most treasured hopes were crushed," though he did not elaborate on what those expectations were. He added, "But I remember that I refused to allow myself to be a victim of any frenzied expression of sadness. I was able to even look at the tears and go on with my life as if nothing was happened."[21[21.

In India, Gandhi struggled to make use of the knowledge he had acquired in London. One reason was that Gandhi did not have a clue about Indian law, and "had no idea of Hindu or Mahomedan law."[22 This was quite understandable, since in England the law school he attended was European law, and did this in order to could get an edge in the fiercely competitive world which represented law in India. But, Gandhi had serious misgivings about whether he'd have the ability to earn money from this occupation. On the advice of a few acquaintances, Gandhi decided to travel to Bombay to get experience with and experience of the High Court and to study Indian law. [23]

Gandhi tried to establish an office of law in Bombay but it was ultimately unsuccessful. He was timid and shy to appear in court, and his timidity resulted in his demise. His first appearance before the Small Causes Court, while interrogating the witness of the plaintiff, Gandhi's mind was blank and he was not able to manage the trial. In the end, he was forced to hand over the brief he received as his first barrister to a friend.

Gandhi did not feel ashamed or ashamed of his shyness. In fact, as per his autobiography, Gandhi came to view his shyness as an advantage "I must admit that, besides the occasional occasions of making me laugh my shyness as a constitutional trait is not a disadvantage at all. In fact , I see that, contrary to what I thought it has been to my benefit. My hesitation in speaking that was previously an issue it is now a joy. The greatest benefit is the fact that I have learned the value of language. I've naturally developed the habit of restricting my thoughts. In fact, I am able to declare to myself that no thoughtless word ever leaves my lips or pen. I don't recall ever regretting something in my writing or speaking. So far, I've avoided many a mistake and a waste of time. My experience has taught me that silence is a part in the practice that is required of an oath of truth. The tendency to exaggerate, or to alter or suppress the truth, either intentionally or without intention is a normal weakness of the human being and silence is a must for overcoming it. A person who speaks only a few words will never be unfocused when speaking He will weigh each word."[24[24.

Recognizing his unsuitability for a court career He resorted to writing applications, and came up with enough money. But, the job was boring and dull and difficult. He was unable to leave this work until 1893, when an Muslim firm from South Africa contacted him, looking for his assistance as an attorney. [25]

Another incident Gandhi called "the the first time I've felt a shock in my entire life" contributed to his disillusionment of his work in his home country, eventually leading him to accept the job to work in South Africa. The elder brother of Gandhi, Laxmidas, had been accused of stealing the state's jewels. The British political agent known as Sir Charles Ollivant was tasked with investigating the allegations and, since Gandhi had been in contact with Ollivant at a meeting in England, Laxmidas asked his brother to intervene.

Gandhi was in conversation with Ollivant and brought up their time together in London. However, Gandhi remembered that "the reminding seemed to tense his shoulders. "Surely you're not coming here to hurt that person has it?' seemed to be...written on his brow."[26]The incident escalated into a fight and ended with an angry British agents taking a physical force to push Gandhi from his workplace. Dissatisfied with the treatment he was given, Gandhi sought out the help of another lawyer who said, "Such things are common experiences. ...[You are fresh from England and are bloody... You don't know British officers."[27]According to Gandhi, "the advice was as bitter as poison...but I had to take it...this education changed the direction of my life."[28]It was probably the first of Gandhi's real encounters with the complexities of inequality, racism and colonialism. it was the first time he saw the full extent of racial arrogance. This was something was not something he encountered while in London. The man also felt humiliated being a law-abiding citizen but not able to challenge the allegations against his brother via formal channels.

Gandhi became increasingly unhappy about his prospects for a career in India. He accepted an offer by an South African firm and thus began to plan his next trip to a different country.

Chapter 2: Gandhi In South Africa

Gandhi in South Africa in 1895

"One thing we've tried to do is observe the most strictest standards that is to never leave the facts in their entirety and, in addressing the complex issues that have been raised in the course of this year, we believe that we've used the most prudent approach possible given the conditions. Our obligation is straightforward and simple. We are here to serve the community and in our humble way, help the Empire. Our faith is in the morality of the cause that is our right to support. We believe in the goodness of the All-powerful God We are steadfastly rooted of that of the British Constitution. This being the case that we cannot fail in our obligation to write anything that was intended to cause harm to. The facts we will always put before our readers, regardless of whether they're palatable to them or not. it's through putting them in front of the public in all their nakedness that the confusion between the two communities of

South Africa can be removed." -- Gandhi, Indian Opinion (1903)

A South African firm initially contacted Gandhi's brother as a legal representative and the response Gandhi got from the company was in the form of: "We have business in South Africa. We are a large company, as well as having a large claim in the Court with our claim of PS40,000. The case has been pending for quite a while. We have enlisted the help of the top barristers and vakils. If you send your brother to this place it would be beneficial to us as well as himself. He could guide us more effectively than we do. He would also benefit from seeing an entirely new region of the globe, and also of making new acquaintances."[2929

Although he was just returning to the city after three weeks spent in London, Gandhi found the deal incredibly appealing. He discussed the conditions and pay with one of its partners, named Dada Abdulla and Co. However, despite the low salary and Gandhi's own admission that the firm was "hardly being employed as barrister ...[butin the role of an employee of the firm" Gandhi accepted the job and came to South Africa in 1893, at the age of 24. [30]

South Africa was to become the pivotal moment for Gandhi. In South Africa, Gandhi was confronted with even more issues, and the process made him a completely different person. Indians living in South Africa were led not by Hindus rather by wealthy Muslims; Hindus in South Africa were mostly servants under indenture living in poverty and obtaining only limited rights. Gandhi's experiences during his time in South Africa exposed him even more to the chasms between different races and ethnicities as well as religions and also the ills of racism.

It's not known what Gandhi was aware of the country which he would spend the next 21 years of his life in. South Africa in the late 1800s and into the mid-1900s was the destination of many poor Indians who arrived on the African continent as laborers under indenture. In the late 1800s and early to mid-1900s, British colonial authorities discovered it was the case that the South

African population was largely economically self-sufficientand did not have the motivation to find work by colonial farmers. This is why the introduction of Indian workers was preferred, even though the social ramifications of such an enormous immigration of foreign workers were not even thought of. [31]

Additionally, South Africa was not one nation. The country's resources and lands were distributed between European powers. Natal to the East was an independent British colony, while Cape in the southwest was a colony of British. Cape to the west was an autonomous British colony, while the interior regions were affected from Dutch and French power. Nationalities, ethnicities, and religions merged and clashed within South Africa, and it was in this context which Indians were taken in as slave laborers in indenture. [32]

Within one week of Gandhi's entry into South Africa, he had an incident that changed the direction in his entire life. On a train that was traveling between Durban to

Pretoria the train stopped and he was kicked out of his first class seat even though he was able to purchase an appropriate ticket at the insistence of a passenger who felt "disturbed" due to the fact that they were an "colored man."[33He was then ejected from the train, and was left with no other choice than to spend the remainder of the night in the waiting area at the Petermaritzburg station, debating whether he should take on his rights and go to Pretoria without a thought of the humiliations, or go back to India. 34 "The suffering that I was subjected to was merely one symptom of the underlying discrimination against people of color," Gandhi wrote of the incident in the autobiography of his. "I must try as much as I can to eliminate the illness and endure some hardships along the way. Redress for wrongs should I pursue only in the amount it is necessary to eliminate the color prejudice."[3535

These experiences of discrimination continued throughout the duration of Gandhi's time. In his journeys to Charlestown the driver of a stagecoach did not allow him to go inside and demanded the driver to sit with him. Although Gandhi was reluctantly acquiesced but when the driver requested that he sit on a floor mat but he declined. The driver began to beat the man and even knocked him off the coach until other passengers were able help him get back to the inside. After a few months, Gandhi was kicked into the sewer by a guard for "daring to pass the residence of President Kruger in Pretoria."[36Gandhi was scolded by names and was slammed in his face. He was subject to racial discrimination on trains.

The struggle began for Gandhi to unify the Indian people of South Africa and fight for their rights. In Pretoria in the year 1897, he convened an assembly of all Indians in the city . He gave them the bleak situations regarding their rights, and liberties, or lack of. The gatherings continued on a regular schedule, and the end result is that "there was at present at Pretoria there was no Indian I had not heard of or whose situation I wasn't familiar with."[37He then contacted railway authorities and insisted that the discrimination Indians endured on trains was not justifiable. He also reached out to his British Agency of Pretoria, Jacobus de Wet whom Gandhi felt had compassion for the Indians but had very no influence to offer any significant assistance. So, Gandhi's time in Pretoria provided him with a profound and thorough understanding of the social, economic and political circumstances of the Indians throughout the surrounding region.

However Gandhi's case in Pretoria which was given by his firm and his firm, was his main engagement in Pretoria. Gandhi was able to study the law regarding the issues at issue and then mediated between both parties, and induced the two sides to reach an agreement to argue in front of an arbitrator. Gandhi was very pleased with the way he handled the case, because he believed that "the real purpose of a lawyer is to bring together parties that were divided asunder."[3838

This was the conclusion of his work as a journalist in South Africa. Gandhi was planning to return to India when, in April 1894, he stumbled upon a brief article in the local newspaper. It was entitled "Indian Franchise," the article discussed a bill which was being discussed by the Natal legislature that would obstruct Indians from having the right to vote. It was suggested that the Indian Franchise Bill could be devastating to the Indian populace's struggle, and Gandhi's own fight for equality of ethnicity for all people in South Africa. Tax exemptions for Indians and other discriminatory practices were in place since the 1980s. However, this outrageous act of discrimination will surely exacerbate the situation of Natal's Indians and, as Gandhi stated that it was the "first nail that was inserted into our coffin."[39After his employer offered at his party to go away to stay for a while in South Africa to help fight the adoption of the bill Gandhi was in agreement and delayed his departure. He quickly transformed the celebration into a work committee , and laid out the foundations for an initiative.

Gandhi selected his to target his campaign in a strategic manner: "the Natal Assembly, which had adopted the Bill as of the time of his campaign; The Europeans of Natal and the those who run the Empire in London as well as the public opinion in India."[40Although the possibility that the bill would be passed was a definite fact prior to when Gandhi and his followers began their campaign, they was successful in helping "infuse fresh vitality into the Indian population," helping it reorganize and redefine its own identity. Gandhi gained the support of every sphere of life who participated in his campaign, including traders, traders, and merchants; Muslims, Hindus, Parsis and Christians as well as the rich and the poor. In his words, Gandhi stated, "We all knew that the passage of this law] was predetermined conclusion however, the agitation brought new life to the community, and had given them the idea that the entire community was inseparable as well equally important to defend its rights to political freedom as its trade rights."[41[41]

Petitions were handed out with thousands of people signing them. collected The campaign also received favorable support from several newspapers which included The Times of India and The London Times. As the campaign progressed into something more extensive and a lot stronger, Gandhi realized that it was now impossible to quit Natal and go back to India. This is why on the 22nd of May in 1894 Gandhi along with a number of supporters established The Natal Indian Congress (NIC) and appointed Gandhi as the party's secretary. From that point until 1906, the work of Gandhi in his campaign was classified as "petition politics" where Gandhi stood up for his convictions predominantly through the writing of petitions, writing articles and organizing support for the community. By his involvement in the public sector, Gandhi was gradually able to organize the Indian community not only in Natal but the entire country across South Africa, into one united political power.

A photo taken at the Natal Indian Congress in 1895

Gandhi's family history as a politician and his education as a lawyer was a huge help in setting up an organized and tightly connected political party. Gandhi was meticulous in keeping the NIC's finances in order and demanded receipts for each donation; "I dare say the account books from 1894 are still intact even in the archives of the Natal Indian Congress," the former president reminisced with pride. Furthermore, Gandhi also established the Colonial-born Indian Educational Association under the under the auspices of the NIC as a group of social members which brought the Natal-born Indian youngsters. The group was described as an "sort of debating society" Gandhi explained that "the Association allowed them to discuss their concerns and issues and stimulate discussion among the members, and also to get them in touch with Indian merchants, and to give the opportunity to serve the community."[44[44]

Another aspect one of NIC was the use of propaganda. The public relations initiatives Gandhi initiated were not restricted in reaching out to Indians in South Africa; he cast more of a net to educate people who were English across South Africa and in England and also Indians in India and in India, with the current situation facing Indians living in South Africa. In this context, Gandhi wrote two pamphlets entitled An

Appeal to every Briton to Every Briton in South Africa and The Indian Franchise A Appeal to the Indian Franchise, which described the conditions that the Indians living in Natal. The pamphlets and the other works were also widely distributed which further elevated Gandhi's name.

In 1894, the exact year that it was the year of Indian Franchise Bill, the Natal government sought to impose a tax per year in the amount of PS25 for indentured Indians. This tax was the result of the inability of European colonizers during the 1860s to account for the economic and social impacts of an enormous population of indentured Indians to South Africa. These Indians were brought to Natal under a five-year agreement and the reward they received was that, at the conclusion of the five-year contract they would have the right to move into Natal and gain complete ownership rights over the land. However, the colonial administration did not consider the long-term effects of this. As the number of indentured servants signed contracts for five years and fulfilled their commitments as they moved to Natal and began to farm their own land , and later adding a range varieties of Indian vegetable varieties that were easy and more affordable to cultivate. Formerly indentured Indians started dominating the agricultural business, and began trading; some could raise their social standing from laborer and farmer to the proprietors of businesses, farms and homes. The sudden threat from the ex-indentured Indians caused alarm among colonial authorities which led them to draft an act to increase taxes on the indentured laborers in order for them to be enticed back to their home country.

Gandhi declared that this was the source of the issue because this development was later expanded into regions of ethnic, racial and religious differences "This (competition with the ex-indentured Indians with white traders] was the seeds of animosity towards Indians. Numerous other factors have contributed to the growth of this conflict. Our various ways of life and our simple lifestyles of life, our satisfaction with small gains, our disinterest in the rules of hygiene and hygiene, our inability to keep our surroundings clean and tidy, as well as our insistence on keeping our homes in good order All these factors, together with the differences in religion have contributed to igniting the flame of animosity. Through legislation, this animosity manifested itself in the bill for disfranchising and in the bill that would impose taxes on indentured Indians. Without legislation, a variety of pinpricks were already started."[46"

Numerous suggestions to expulse Indian laborers or forcibly return them were tossed out and rejected in the Natal government, after which the Indian government refused to accept them. Therefore the Natal government chose to tax indentured Indians to accelerate their removal of South Africa, or encourage them to leave South Africa when their five-year contracts were expiring. The tax proposal was astonished Gandhi as well as the Indian population, since just one pound per individual would've destroyed the lives of families that had a salary of less than fourteen seventy shillings per month. And there were plenty of families like that in Natal. The NIC led a vigorous campaign against taxation but was unable to remove the tax. In the Viceroy's office, India accepted a three-pound levy for every former-indentured Indian within Natal. [47]

Gandhi continued to work, but he did take a few days off during 1896 to return his home in India. When Gandhi came back to Durban in December 1896, this time with his children and wife along to Durban, officials in Durban, who recognized Gandhi initially denied the Indian passenger's entry. They also requested the captain of the ship to take the ship back to India. The captain as well as the passengers refused to go until the beginning of January 1897, Gandhi as well as his fellow passengers were granted entry.

The next day would be a terrifying incident for Gandhi but he was not the only one. Many had advised him not to go out without covering his tracks, since the disdain of the European people for Gandhi was very high, and his life was at risk. As he had been cautioned, Gandhi was attacked by an armed group of white youngsters, and was able to escape through the help from the spouse of the police superintendent of

Durban. A few years later, Gandhi wrote of his delight at the strength that he displayed when he was confronted by the crowd: "God has always come to my rescue...My determination stood up to the stern test on the 13th of January, 1897 when...I set out to sea and was confronted by the mob of screaming people determined to lynch me. I was surrounded by thousands them...but my strength was never a problem. I'm not sure how courage came to me. It did. God is great."[4848

Then, Gandhi was asked by Harry Escombe, an influential South African statesman who was one of the most prominent cabinet members in Natal's and asked if he wanted to bring his attackers to justice He replied, "I do not want to pursue anyone. It's possible that I could be capable of identifying some couple of the suspects, but what's the point of having the culprits punished? In addition, I don't consider the attackers to be the cause. They were made aware that I been making exaggerated claims in India regarding the whites of Natal and vilified them. If they believed the reports then it's no wonder that they were angry. The leaders, and in the event that I am allowed to state it I am blaming you. You could have led the people in the right way however, it seems that you also...assumed that I overstated the situation. I don't want to charge anyone. I'm certain that once the truth is exposed the person will feel sorry for their conduct."[4949

The events mentioned above and many others throughout his life demonstrate his complete understanding of who his real adversaries were. Gandhi believed the perpetrators weren't to blame, but those responsible were the ones who led the attackers and created the tension within which they lived. Many other incidents from Gandhi's life, as well as his reaction to them illustrate this. When he was detained from the train following being required to leave his first class seat, he didn't take the blame for the black passenger that informed the train conductor or security guards who kicked his off, but rather the railway company or the highest authorities that allowed the prejudicial act to continue.

Before he realized the severity of discrimination as well as racism, Gandhi was fully aware of who and what had to be taken down to make a system change, but the Gandhi was increasingly aware that campaigns and petitions that included writing, propaganda and rational persuasion were having an insignificant impact on the current situation. On the 22nd of August 1906 The Transvaal Government Gazette published the draft of the Asiatic Law Amendment Ordinance, which required to everyone Indians, Arabs, and Turks to be registered in the official system. The process involved taking fingerprints and recording the identification marks of individuals' bodies, in order to issue an official certification of their registration. A fine of up to 100 pounds or three months' in prison, is imposed for those who did not sign up by the specified date. The proposed law was a shock to the majority of foreigners living within South Africa, and the law was referred to in the form of the "Black Act" in the eyes of the Indians. [50]

The Black Act exceedingly discriminatory, it was also deeply humiliating. The Indians and other populations from outside were required to pass the registration process that was expected by common criminals. Gandhi quickly called a massive gathering of 3000 Indians in September 11th, 1906 and announced what became to be called the fourth resolution that was adopted by the group. The resolution demanded protest against the Black Act through civil disobedience which included arrest and detention in the event of need. Gandhi was clear the people he was supporting that the resolution was not like the other resolutions that the NIC had adopted previously: "It is a very important resolution we are makingbecause our very existence within South Africa depends upon our adhering to it."[51[51

Images from Gandhi in 1906

A few years after that Gandhi spoke of the events of this gathering in the context of an "advent of the satyagraha (truth)," and these concepts became fundamental elements of Gandhi's thought and practice.

The first is the argument that inequity is not just discriminatory and unfair , but also humiliating because it deprives Indians from their respectability and self-esteem. Gandhi's subsequent calls of swaraj (freedom) by satyagraha the result of his efforts at that gathering, in which Gandhi was a vocal advocate for a new confidence in self-esteem and self-confidence within the Indian people from South Africa. [52]

The result of this meeting was the beginning of what became known as "passive resist," an expression of non-violent resistance, which included peaceful protests and picketing at register centers. It also involved burning registration documents, courting arrests and humbly accepting all sentences or punishments which were handed down to the detained. But, Gandhi disliked the term "passive resistance" since it implied insecurity and weakness. He prefer "active non-violent protest against injustice" rather. [53]

One of Gandhi's biographers said, "What Gandhi did to South Africa...was less significant than how South Africa did to him."[54[54] South Africa provided the laboratory for Gandhi's experimentation with the concepts of self-rule and freedom and peaceful protest, and consequently, proved to be an excellent test-bed, since many of the issues the man faced there were echoed in India. In South Africa that Gandhi took his years of thinking of childhood wonder, memories and frustrations, and consolidated the ideas into a firm foundation. He was influenced by the three years of law school in London as well as the diversity of religion and ethnicity which he witnessed in England as well as South Africa, and the racism he experienced in this new land and turned these experiences into a quest for himself as well as for India. As one biographer of him Dennis Dalton, "This mission was one of self-realization. However, prior to leaving South Africa he knew that it would require a fight to secure India's freedom, too. He quit Bombay to go to Durban in 1893 to be counsel to the legal department of Dada Abdulla and Company; He returned to India twenty-one years later , with the feeling of mission and a wealth of experiences in political and social reform and the ideals that were the basis for his political thinking. This is the kind of thing that South Africa did for Gandhi."[55[55]

Gandhi's call to peaceful protests in opposition to the Black Act led to some concessions that ultimately did not meet the protesters demand. The protests were repeated a few years later, this time involving Indian miners and women who were protesting not just against the discriminatory act , but as well against the inability by the government to acknowledge Indian marriages, unfair restrictions on immigration, as well as the system that discriminates against labor indentured. The movement was led by Gandhi thousands of Indian women marched illegally across borders from Transvaal to the Natal coalfields and convinced the miners to strike. Security forces were brought into the area, and after Gandhi and his protesters were brutally penalized, the national and international protests led the then-Prime Secretary Jan Smuts to reach out to Gandhi to discuss discussions. The negotiations that followed resulted in an agreement known as the Smuts-Gandhi Agreement on June 30 in 1914, as well as the passing of the Indian Relief Act of 1914. This Act was a major achievement in the eyes of Gandhi and his followers, since it addressed two important concerns Gandhi was fighting for the past decade: the tax of 3 pounds which was imposed upon Indians who failed to renew their indentures, as well as the refusal of the state to acknowledge Indian marriages. The Act eliminated taxes and recognized the legitimacy for Indian traditional marriages. [56]

Gandhi as well as his spouse were in South Africa in 1914

The victory, as well as his whole experience during his time in South Africa altered Gandhi's life. Like I said the 21 years spent in the foreign country had a profound impression on him, an effect he could not have had doing law in India. The South Africa experience led to the realization that the path to success is nonviolent resistance or the satyagraha. He also realized that thought and life were interdependent. Gandhi recognized that thinking was useless if it wasn't applied in real life, and that life had no significance unless one had thought about what his ideal of a life that was meaningful.

It was it was in South Africa that Gandhi began following the rules of an ascetic way of life that would eventually become one of his main methods that were admired and replicated across the world. In his autobiography under the heading of "Simple Life" Gandhi recalled that he discovered his "beauty that self-help can bring" after the time came to wash his own clothes in hand, thereby reducing the cost of laundry. [57] Gandhi added the fact that the "passion for self-help, and the simplicity" was born with South Africa; the seed was planted and "it just needed watering in order to grow, to bloom and then to mature then the watering began in its proper course."[58[58]

Chapter 3: Gandhi And The Indian Independence Movement

Gandhi in 1915

"I consider that the culture India has developed cannot be defeated anywhere in the world. It is impossible to match the seeds planted by our ancestors. Rome was gone, Greece shared the same destiny; the power of the Pharaohs was shattered. Japan has been Westernized and of China it is impossible to speak yet India remains, in some way or another, solid at the base of its civilization. People in Europe are learning by reading the works of men from Greece or Rome that are not in their previous splendor. When they attempt to take lessons from their mistakes the Europeans believe that they can not make the same mistakes as Greece or Rome. This is the pity of them. Within this, India remains unmovable, and that's what she is known for." -- Gandhi, Hind Swaraj (1908)

Gandhi left India in 1893 when he was an unexperienced, young and timid lawyer, unsure what his next steps would be. In 1914, he returned to South Africa as a person who was reborn, confident as well as proud and knowledgeable and with a strong cause within his heart. The man was who had an international reputation as a prominent Indian nationalist activist, rights advocate, and leader. So when his ship arrived in Bombay in the month of January, Gandhi as well as his spouse received a warm welcome from the crowd as the announcement of the return of his Indian heroes from South Africa had spread across the nation. When journalists inquired about his plans to return to India, Gandhi humbly replied that he'd spend sometime as an "observer as well as a student" because he had plenty to know about political system of the country he had spent more than two years. For at least one year, he planned to take some time to adjust in Indian life. One of his biographers stated, "He'd promised his political mentor, Gokhale, that he'd not make any political declarations in the upcoming time, not take sides, and not engage in any moves. He would travel across the country to establish connections to be known, listen and be observant. In more esoteric terms one could see him as an attempt to take in the vastness of Indian real-world as possible. It was much more than any other actor in the Indian scene has ever attempted."[6060

In the midst of the fame he earned through his struggle for justice in South Africa, Gandhi was invited to tea parties, and even talks where he was celebrated as an hero. Gandhi's usual response was to decline such praise and instead focus on those who were the "real the heroes" those who were indentured labourers from South Africa. He continued to travel around his country, with "his ears shut and mouth open," he came to draw two important conclusion. [62]

The second was that even although there was no public and unambiguous protest against colonial rule, there was a sense of a strong dislike for the oppressive British rule over the Indian populace. The author also noted the fact that, in 1885, political organizations had risen to protest colonialism, one of them being those of the Indian National Congress being the most popular but, the Congress which was established in 1885, proved to be largely ineffective, mostly because of its "begging and humiliating" tactics. On the other side in the spectrum of terrorist groups have emerged, using violence and threats in an attempt to effect changes in the political system. While Gandhi was a part of the ferocity of these movements as well as demands for action immediately however, he was strongly opposed to the violent tactics they employed on practical and moral reasons. Gandhi was aware, as he had experienced in Natal that violence did not bring about real lasting change and even more detrimental because it eroded at the morality of combatants. Also, violence made it difficult to build self-confidence, courage and a sense of collective action amongst the masses because fear stifled any real unity. This is why Gandhi believed that the satyagraha method that he devised and tried through South Africa was India's best chance.

The second point Gandhi offered was a larger one. He concluded, after a considerable amount of hours of study of the people of his nation and their history, that they were in an "degenerate" state because of years of colonialism and foreign rule. 64 Indians had been thrown into chaos that was deeply divided due to impassable caste walls, a myriad of religious groups, and ethnicities. There was a severe absence of social conscience and morality, and instead the population was self-centered, insecure and downright demoralized. Gandhi recognized that the most important issue his nation needed was not independence of the British or self-independence. India was in need of being re-energized and revived before it could gain independence, or even keep the status it had once it achieved.

So, Gandhi began working out an extensive program for national revitalization known as"The Constructive Program. The program was developed based on the belief that creating an entirely new society within the ruins of the previous was a major, non-violent, social change , a re-construction of society. Political expert Robert Burrowes explained in his study, The Strategy of Nonviolent Defense The Strategy of

Nonviolent Defense: A Gandhian Methodology the Gandhian Constructive Program was founded on the notion of "non-violence...was more than an approach to fight or a way to resist the military's aggression." As per Burrowes the Gandhian principle of non-violence was "intimately connected to the larger struggle for justice and social equity as well as economic self-reliance and ecological harmony, as well as the pursuit of the realization of oneself." This conviction and the conviction of Gandhi to be successful, his Constructive Program along with the method of non-violent defense it was founded on "required rebuilding the social, personal economic, political, and personal life of every individual."[65So, according to Gandhi his beliefs, improvements and reconstruction were not only the responsibility for the community but also of the individual "for each individual. It meant greater ability to control oneself through the development of the individual's identity, self-reliance and confidence," while "for the community, it was the creation of a brand new set of social, political and economic relations."[66[66.]

So, Gandhi was well aware that a change in regime wasn't the sole thing needed to see an India that was reborn. In the past there have been many instances of revolutions led by political leaders in countries where the populace was not organized or capable of exercising their own autonomy which resulted in was a swift return to the dictatorial system. To stop this from happening in India the Indian people first must strengthen their unity and then, collectively, start an asocial revolution along with an electoral one.

The Constructive Program included small and big items that dealt with different aspects of living. It also included proposals Gandhi considered to be "absolutely vital," such as Hindu-Muslim unity, a prohibition of alcohol as well as the use of Khadi (hand-spun hand-woven cloth) and the creation of local industries, as well as crafts-based education. Other fundamental concepts included equal rights for women, health education, the adoption of a common language, equality of economic opportunity and the development of peasants' and unions of workers and organizations as well as the inclusion of tribal people to mainstream society. [67]

Certain of these ideas were more directly connected to the development of Indian society than others, however they were all crucial to the progress. For instance, the introduction of khadi could seem unimportant and unimportant, but its purpose was to create a uniform for the nation and provide a degree of equality. Gandhi's goal was to instill the feeling of a united solidarity with the less fortunate and to create economic pressure on the British and reduce the imports of foreigners. In the same way, the introduction of a common language was intended to bring together the wide and diverse differences between religious, ethnic and social groups in India and to widen the divide between nationalist people and those who were Westernized elite. The creation of local industries was designed to not just help the poor and disadvantaged in the rural areas as well as to reduce the process of transferring into cities. [68 It was the Constructive Program became an essential part of Gandhi's struggle to secure Indian freedom.

When he was developing his Constructive Plan, Gandhi understood that he needed a platform from which to speak and for his voice to be heard. In the end, the Indian National Congress was the most popular political party in India even though it was largely unsuccessful to achieve its goals. Gandhi was reluctant joining any political organization following the time he returned back to India in 1915, however by 1918, he had back and willing to get involved in politics. He then became a member of in the Indian National Congress party, however, he found his position to be inadequate. To improve it, in 1919 Gandhi tried to expand his support base as well as extend his appeal to the Muslim populace of India.

The chance was presented through the Khilafat movement that was a pan-Islamic political protest that was launched in the name of Muslims across India to protest against the demise of the Ottoman Caliphate (Islamic state) in Turkey following the Second World War. Gandhi offered his support to its leaders and urged the establishment of an well-organized, non-violent, and non-violent, organization of non-cooperation. The leaders agreed which was in the month of June, 1920. they established the official Khilafat movement. Gandhi demanded the leaders in the Indian National Congress to support the Khilafat movement. Gandhi's popularity as an one of the more popular public speakers of the movement led to him receiving substantial Muslim support. This is how Gandhi made history as the only leader of national significance to lead a nation in India with a multi-cultural and multiethnic base of support, which helped him climb to higher positions that had influence within Congress. Even though by 1922 in 1922, Khilafat had dissolved, Khilafat movement had fallen apart, Gandhi had become a prominent leader of Congress. Indian National Congress. [69]

In the autumn in 1920 Gandhi became the most powerful persona of the party, gaining the power that has not ever been achieved by a politician in India. He changed the structure of his party, the Indian National Congress by transforming it from a group comprised predominantly of upper middle class elites to a nationalist party that had roots in villages and rural towns. Under Gandhi's direction the constitution was revised with a focus on non-violence or threats Gandhi promoted non-violent, non-cooperative action against the British and British-owned companies, as well as an outright boycott against British manufacturing companies and British-owned institutions like courts, legislatures offices, schools and the legislature. The membership was open to all and the party was made open to everyone who could afford a nominal fee. The elitism that was visible in the party was completely eradicated and was replaced by an organisation with popularity across the country.

In the year 1920, Gandhi and the Congress began a new program dubbed"the Non-Cooperation Movement. In accordance with the principles of Gandhi and his followers, the Congress changed its focus from achieving self-government via legal and constitutional means in order to achieve an swaraj (independence) by non-cooperation or nonviolence and peaceful resistance. Among its main principles were: the surrendering of titles and honors; boycott of government and government-affiliated schools and colleges, courts, and foreign clothes; resignation from government services; and mass civil disobedience, including the non-payment of taxes. The program of the movement emphasized several of the principles embraced in the Constructive Program of Gandhi through his Constructive Program which included the promotion and acceptance of khadi, the Hindu-Muslim union as well as a strict adherence to non-violence. [70]

Gandhi as well as Indian poet Rabindranath Tagore in 1920.

The movement was able to gain widespread support across the country, particularly for youths and students. Gandhi and other members of the Congress undertook a nationwide tour, lecturing to the masses and encouraging the building of national schools and colleges while calling for the boycott of government-affiliated institutions. As a result many students quit their schools to join national institutions which were created in this time; an estimate of 800 establishments were created in the course of this period. People also were against foreign clothing and other products and shops that sold foreign products as well as liquor were snubbed and beaten, while those who supported them burnt foreign clothing in public. Imports of foreign goods dropped drastically.

The reaction of the British crown was harsh. The government detained Congress leaders, but Gandhi was not arrested, and put strict restrictions on press freedom while prohibiting public meetings that were not authorized. On February 19, 1922 just as the movement was approaching its peak, it was abruptly stopped after a violent confrontation took place within the city of Chauri Chaura in which the protesters demanding non-cooperation became violent and set fire to the police station. Deaths of innocent civilians as well as policemen resulted in Gandhi declaring the end of the national protest. Instead, he urged his supporters to participate in constructive endeavors like promoting the khadi, creating national institutions and encouraging the unity of Hindus and Muslims. [72]

The sudden demise of the movement created a lot of confusion and critique. Opponents and supporters alike challenged the wisdom of Gandhi in deciding to end the movement. But, Gandhi had realized several crucial things during this time The first was that the population was not yet ready for a non-violent political system. In his Constructive Program in order for society to transform, the people that comprised them also needed undergo self-analysis, self-improvement and change. On the practical side this Chauri Chaura incident may easily led to another violent incident If this were to happen, the entire Non-Cooperation Movement would have been condemned and considered unlegitimate. Then, Gandhi also realized that the movement, following its initial rage, was now at the point of no return. Gandhi realized the challenges of maintaining enthusiasm and enthusiasm in a large-scale protest for an extended period of time.

However it is true that the Non-Cooperation Movement played a large contribution to enhancing Gandhi's acclaim and enlarged the reach of the Indian National Congress of influence when it won the trust and support that of millions Indians across all segments of society. Additionally, the population from India initially were able to experiment with organizing and mass mobilization. Through it being the Non-Cooperation Movement, the people could show that they were able to participate in a national-wide, unison mass movement, regardless of their ethnicity and social standing or the religion of their choice.

After a few weeks of putting an end to the protest, Gandhi was arrested on March 10, 1922. He was charged with sedition, which resulted in a sentence of six years of imprisonment. The central person's sudden deportation caused immediately disorganization and confusion within the leadership and members of Congress. The Congress was divided between those who sought to make a change immediately and those who didn't and the "pro-changers" wanted on the issuing of a cease-and-desist order to government's boycott and wanted to be able to vote. The "pro-changers" ended up resigning out of Congress at the beginning of January in 1923, and formed their own party, dubbed Swaraj Party. Swaraj Party. In the elections for the council in November 1923 the Swaraj Party was able to get an impressive 42 of 100 seats in the Imperial Legislative Councils. As a result of this party division, the cooperation between Hindus and Muslims was also breaking in the absence of Gandhi as the leader.

Gandhi got released on February 19, 1924 after serving just the two-year portion of his sentence. Through in the 20th century, Gandhi was largely out of the spotlight of politics, focusing instead on reforms to the inner ring by trying to heal the divide among both the Congress as well as Swaraj Party. Swaraj Party, but this was changed in 1927 in which the British government established an constitutional reform commission headed by Sir John Simon, a prominent politician and lawyer. The reform commission didn't include one Indian member, which led to protests throughout India. Sir John Simon arrived in India in the month of November 1927. However, there were protests and boycotts everywhere he was. The Congress as well as various other parties opposed the Commission. On December 28, 1928 during the Congress party's Calcutta session, Gandhi pushed through a resolution calling on to the British crown to give India the status of a dominion within a year period, or else face another campaign of opposition with full autonomy for India as its ultimate goal. This resolution came out of Gandhi's efforts to bridge the gap between different opinions within the Congress particularly between demands for an immediate declaration of independence as well as calls for more patience. [73]

The British did not respond. A year later on December 31, 1929 India's flag India was raised in Lahore and the 26th of January of 1930 was declared the country's Independence Day by the Congress's session in Lahore. In the Lahore session also announced that the goal of the Congress to be full independence. And after the declaration, it declared the start in the civil disobedience known as Non-Cooperation movement. In addition the Lahore session also granted permission to Gandhi to lead the new movement. Gandhi delivered an ultimatum of sorts to the British government with a list of eleven demands and gave the British up to January 31, 1930 to make their response. The demands Gandhi made included complete prohibition, freedom of prisoners from political prison; changes within the Criminal Investigation Department; and the abolishment of salt taxes as well as the monopoly of the state on salt. The British refused to comply with the demands.

Gandhi was the reason for an act that is among his infamous actions The Salt Satyagraha, also known as the Salt March or Dandi March which took place in March of 1930. From the beginning of March until early the month of April Gandhi took a walk of nearly two hundred miles, from Ahmedabad to Dandi in protest of Salt Tax, with the intention of making salt by himself when he got to the ocean. Gandhi started his march at Ahmedabad with 78 of his followers of all castes and religions and was followed by thousands of supporters during the march. When Gandhi arrived at the ocean in Dandi on the 6th of April 1930, he snatched up the salt in outright defiance to the ban of the government, and formally launched the movement. In the Indian coast many people, mostly peasants from in the area, followed his lead and made salt in violation. The salt marches resulted in the arrest for more than 60, 000 persons who took part in the marches. [75]

Images of Gandhi taking part at the Salt March

The satyagraha was vital to Gandhi's campaign. It convinced the nation and the world that the colonial system was in danger, and that the people could stop it by uniting with the colonial government, and also exposed the brutality of the colonial regime to the majority all of humanity. The march resulted in internationalizing this Indian struggles for their independence, making to the British government to international pressure. The embarrassment the British government had to endure was serious; there had never during the course of its dominance over India been such a large number of Indians being imprisoned and, as Gandhi was at this time an international person whose every move was the talk of the town His imprisonment because he snatched a handful salt pushed Britain to take on more pressure.

The protests continued and led to the government finally committing to start talks with Gandhi. Gandhi was invited across London in the role of solely representing the Indian National Congress and accepted an agreement to cease fire, but was shocked to learn that the issue of independence for India wasn't even the subject of debate. Furthermore after Gandhi came back in India the month of December, 1931, Gandhi discovered his party victimized by one of the most severe government-imposed repressions that the nationalism movement has ever experienced. Gandhi was detained again, together with the top members from the Congress. The government, refusing to engage from discussions, instead isolated Gandhi and tried to limit its influence through keeping him disregarded by his supporters and the general public. The Congress and every activity associated with it was banned and restrictions were placed on the press.

The year 1934 was when Gandhi was finally able to end the civil disobedience movement twice. Similar to the first the previous time, he was finding it difficult to lead an all-national movement. In the same year Gandhi quit as the leader and a member of the Congress. He was beginning to feel at this time that his party's members did not adhere to his tenets for nonviolence, a basic and vital necessity however, they had only used it as a way to increase their popularity. Instead of focusing on the politics, Gandhi now concentrated fully on his Constructive Program to build a better nation through promoting the fundamentals of his program and transforming society from the bottom up. [76]

In 1939, when World War II broke out in 1939, Gandhi initially called for giving moral and non-violent aid to the British military. The Congress also supported backing Britain as long as the country's independence was guaranteed. The British stated that following the conflict, a constituency assembly would be created to decide the future structure of politics in India. But to Gandhi as well as the Congress as well as the majority of India the promise was not enough. They demanded immediate talks for the nation's independence. India and asserted that India was not able to support an army that claims to fight for freedom of the democratic, even as it was fighting for its freedom. The British government was unable to provide adequate responses, which led to the Congress's refusal of assistance for the war effort of Britain.

Gandhi in 1939

But, the incredible success achieved by Adolf Hitler gained in the war caused Britain and allies to seek help from India. The month of August, 1940 was when Britain offered India with plans for constitutional reforms in India. The proposal was referred to as the August offer, the principal provisions included: India was to receive dominion status, the British Viceroy's executive committee would be expanded, and after the war, a constituency assembly comprised mostly of Indians would be created to determine the new Indian constitution. The Congress quickly turned down the offer, arguing that the proposed dominion status was not acceptable It was either complete independence or no. Gandhi also opposed the August Offer and demanded the launching the limited Satyagraha which was later known as the "individual Satyagraha" which was limited to a small number of chosen individuals from each community were permitted to lead Satyagraha in the form of speeches in opposition to the war as well as public declarations of opposition to Britain. The people chosen by Gandhi to conduct this particular satyagraha had to notify officials in advance of the date and venue of the planned anti-war speech. [77]

The goal of this satyagraha differed than the earlier protests. It was designed to address directly the issue in question, this particular satyagraha was designed to demonstrate clearly that even though India was not a supporter of Hitler or Nazism but it was not able to be forced to join the military efforts of Britain which is limiting its own rights. The movement was started in protest of Gandhi's conviction that, in the end there was no difference in the world between Nazism or the autocracy that doubled that was imposed on India. Over 25 satyagrahis were taken into custody, sentenced and imprisoned for their participation in the movement. [78In fact, Gandhi believed that their sacrifices were worthy of the cause, and the movement gained widespread acceptance and international attention.

On March 22, 1942 while the war was raging in the second half of 1942, it was the time that British Government sent India their House of Commons leader, Stafford Cripps, with a set of ideas to win the support of India to the British efforts to win the war. In response to Japan's decision of supporting Germany during the war and the attack on Pearl Harbor in December 1941 The Cripps plan was seen as a last ditch bid to save the country to gain ground during one of the biggest conflicts in the history of. The principal aspects of the proposal were : the establishment of one Indian Union with dominion status and the formation of a constituent body post-WWII to create a new constitution; and the appointment of representatives from Indian princes to the assembly. The Cripps mission's proposal was rebuffed due to a variety of reasons, including Congress which included objections to dominion status as well as the call for total independence; fair and free elections for members of the constituent assembly There were no discussions or guarantees regarding the the transfer of powers. Gandhi declared his opposition to the plan and called it an "post-dated check for an insolvent bank."[79[79]

Cripps

Stafford Cripps returned to England without a deal with the British, and Gandhi declared to the British must "Quit India," and India should start an all-new struggle of disobedience to the state in order to bring the message home. In July 1942, the Congress Working Committee met in July 1942 and approved the idea for a second battle in the mass by adopting the Quit India Resolution that was approved on August 8th on the 8th of August, 1942. The resolution demanded an immediate end to British rule and the complete independence for India and the promise that a liberated India will stand up and defend itself against any fascist or imperialist forces. This threat came from: should the British were not willing to comply with these demands in the resolution, the Congress declared it would initiate an act of civil disobedience under the direction of Gandhi. The intention from Congress was that Congress was that no nation fighting for its own survival - especially when the war tides were shifting in the direction of the British - would accept this kind of disturbance, no matter how non-violent.

The Congress was correct The threat of another campaign of civil disobedience India was too for the Indian government. In the early day of the 9th August in 1942 saw Gandhi as well as all the prominent members of the Congress were detained and detained in unidentified places. Since the arrests took place shortly after the announcement of Quit India movement, neither Gandhi or the Congress leaders had the chance to plan any sort of protest. With no direction, protesters escalated into violence, resulting in incidents of violence across several regions of India where people smashed trains, destroyed structures as well as bridges and state property. The violent crowds cut the telegraph lines and attacked police stations and erected flags on public buildings. Students walked out of their classes, and workers struck. The government was savage and nearly 60,000 people were detained, the police were fired more than 538 times and nearly 940 were killed in the tense violence. [82]

A photo of Gandhi writing in 1942.

Gandhi went on to spend the next two years in jail along with the majority of Congress leaders. Much to Gandhi's sorrow his wife Kasturbai was detained in a different place was killed in jail. "I can't imagine my life without her,"" Gandhi said of her passing away. "We were with her for sixty two years...nothing can fill the gap in my life."[83The new Viceroy Lord Wavell was the one who wrote Gandhi his condolence letter that deeply touched Gandhi. Six weeks after the death of his wife, Gandhi fell so severely sick that the Viceroy was able to release him in fear of the outcry that could be generated should Gandhi died in prison. It was the last period that Gandhi was ever detained. In India the country, he was sentenced to 298 years in the prison. [84]

While Congress members were imprisoned while the other parties in politics, including that of Muslim League, strategically played their part and supported the British efforts to win their support. It was headed by Muhammad Ali Jinnah, from the time of the conflict in the early years, the Muslim League was insisting on self-determination for the Muslim populace in India and at the 1940 meeting at Lahore, Jinnah stated that "The Mussalmans [Muslims] are not an ethnic minority...The Mussalmans are a nation...The issue with the problem in India is not an inter-communal nature, but clearly of an international nature, and should be treated as such."[85]Thus with the intention of bringing together the whole Muslim populace, Jinnah introduced a language of nationalist religious sentiment into the discussion of Indian independence, which drastically altered the character of the debate. From then on Jinnah spoke of Muslims as a people who had the right to complete self-determination and equal status as the Hindus even though it was the case that Jinnah as well as the Muslim League were arguing for a long time that the Muslim was an independent Muslim group within of the Indian nation. Jinnah then called for British to transfer their post-war power , not to one single India and not to any of the "autonomous nation states" from south-east Asia. South Asian continent, delineating his ideas for the new nation of Pakistan. [86]

One of Gandhi's enduring convictions was that of Hindu-Muslim unity which is why, naturally, Gandhi was strongly opposed to any form of partition. The partition plan was branded as an "untruth," Gandhi insisted that there should be "no compromise" with it...Does Islam bind Muslim only to Muslim and oppose those who are Hindu? Did the message of the Prophet peace only between

Muslims and the war against Hindus or non-Muslims? ?...Those who have infused this poison in the Muslim mind do the most harm to Islam. I'm sure it's not Islam."[87[87

But Jinnah as well as the Muslim League gained significant organizational power during the war, as their rival and ally, the Congress which was brutally crushed. In the event that Britain and allies prevailed and ended the war in 1945 and a new chapter in Indo-British ties began when an entirely new British government, which was governed by the Labour Party that had come to power following the war, declared it would grant the independence of India.

Chapter 4: Of Gandhi's End Years

"Truth is the only thing that will last and all other things will disappear in the course of time. I must keep on bearing the testimony of truth, even when I am disregarded by everyone. My voice may be today an unheard voice in the wilderness however, you will hear it even when the other voice is silenced in the case that they are the voices of Truth." Gandhi Gandhi

On the 15th of August, 1946 Muhammad Ali Jinnah called for an "Direct Act Day." What was meant by such an event was not clear at first however, the announcement was immediately then followed by violent protests and violence. Muslims were killed by Hindus in large numbers in the midst of several days of chaos Hindus returned the favor and began attacking Muslims. The killings led to revenge murders villages were burnt, children and women were murdered as the country sank into chaos. The conflict between Muslims and Hindus caused a lot of grief to Gandhi profoundly. Gandhi went on a half-fast and ate only 600 calories per day in protest of the massacres. He promised to stay on this fast until the violence ended, and then he walked between villages to talk about the brotherly bond. A month later the killings ended after "his body diminished to the shadow of its previous self."[89[89]

As Gandhi was protesting against the murders and visiting villages after villages and visiting village after village, his fellow members of the Congress, Muslim League, and Viceroy were engaged in secret talks in Delhi to create a new division in India. Gandhi wasn't consulted during the negotiations and, probably would have preferred not to be included in these discussions because he was of the opinion that a divided India was not an India in the first place. Although the Viceroy finally urged him to visit Delhi, Gandhi politely declined and knew that his request was solely in respect. On August 15th, 1947 the Viceroy transferred the power in an unindependent India and the newly-created the state of Pakistan. [90]

Prior to the separation, Gandhi had spent years in debate and argument with Jinnah. He was totally different from Gandhi in terms of personality, thinking and behavior - he was a complex man, rude and distant. Both men had common ancestors, since Jinnah was from the same area of India as Gandhi was from, had the same language and cultural values and was a lawyer and his family was one of the first generations of Hindu converts. In spite of having the advantage of knowing that Gandhi throughout his life had managed to win over many powerful foreign and Indian individuals, Gandhi ultimately "failed before the man who was close his own in many ways than his rivals. opponents."[91[91]

Gandhi along with Jinnah during Bombay in 1944.

Gandhi lived in Calcutta when the partition of India and the declaration of independence for India were made. The body was weak after the fast, Gandhi settled in the areas of slums and confronted the mob in the slums, pleading for peace: "They insulted him, hit him with bricks and spat on him, and hurled insults at him. In his own company, the small man dressed in a loincloth and steel-rimmed glasses stood firm and spoke to the crowd and not paying attention to their conduct, and at time, following couple of days, the streets were still. Gandhi was the only person who created an amazing miracle. In Punjab in India, where the Viceroy deployed fifty thousand army soldiers in an effort to stop the people from killing one another 350,000 people were murdered , and fourteen million ran away. In Bengal thanks to Gandhi's presence, no one was killed and no one fled. According to the Viceroy"What fifty million well-equipped soldiers can't do it, the Mahatma has accomplished and brought peace. He is a single person army .'"[92[]

Gandhi and the final British Viceroy of the United Kingdom, Lord Mountbatten In 1947.

After separation, India as well as Pakistan entered into war over the status of Kashmir. Gandhi announced a last fast - the 20th day of his life - to ensure the end of the war and for the security of Muslims in India. The news of Gandhi's fast spread quickly and, when it was heard by extremist Hindus and Hindus, threats of death were issued to Gandhi because of his apparent support for Muslims against Hindus. [93] On the 30th of January 1948 Mahatma Gandhi was killed by an unidentified young Hindu nationalist who was attending an assembly of prayer at New Delhi. Nathuram Godse, the assassin was a member of extreme Hindu Mahasabha, an ultra-right nationalist group that was adamantly opposed to Gandhi's nonviolence stance and a strong supporter of Muslims as well as Pakistan. The Prime of the country Jawaharlal Nehru was Gandhi's closest adviser and friend, spoke to the nation on radio to announce his beloved friend's passing: "Friends and comrades, the light has been sucked out of our lives and there is darkness everywhere. I'm not sure what I should say or how to convey the words. The beloved and revered leader of our nation, Bapu who we call the father of our nation, is gone. It is possible that I am incorrect in saying that; however we will never be seeing him as the times we've seen him throughout all these years. We are not going to Bapu for advice or seek for comfort from him. that's a huge blownot just to myself, but for millions of people across this country."[94[94]

Gandhi as well as Nehru in 1942

Nathuram Godse

Wilson Loo Kok Wee's photograph of the memorial that marks the spot of Gandhi's assassination.

Many people took part in Mahatma Gandhi's funeral, and were able to join in the funeral procession of five miles. The mourning was a common theme in India, Pakistan, and throughout the world. All Indian institutions in London closed in the early morning as hundreds of Hindus, Muslims, and different races, religions and religious groups from across Britain attended the funeral in the India House located in London. In the aftermath of his passing, sorrow overcame the hearts and minds of all violent protesters who refused to comply with Gandhi's call to peaceful protest. The massacres were stopped quickly and across India flags were raised at half-masts to honor Mohandas Karamchand Gandhi, who was, as an American politician called him, "the spokesman of the conscience of mankind."[96The spokesman of the conscience of mankind.

Chapter 5: Gandhi's Practiques And Beliefs

"I consider that peace is far superior to violence. Forgiveness will be more manly and wholesome than punishment forgiveness is a beautiful thing to wear on a soldier. However, abstinence only works when it is possible to punish, and it's useless when it claims to be the perspective of a helpless animal. A mouse doesn't forgive cat when it lets itself to be ripped apart by her. ... The truth is that I am not convinced that I be an unhelpful creature. But I do want to harness India's strength and India's to achieve a greater goals. Don't misunderstand me. The strength of a person is not the result of physical strength. It is the result of an unbreakable determination." -- Gandhi

The numerous concepts and ways of Gandhi have come to be referred to as Gandhism. Although many of his ideas were heavily influenced and influenced by religions - not only his own Hinduism however, but also Christianity, Judaism, and Jainism He was also greatly influenced by the work of great philosophers like Plato and Thoreau and the author Leo Tolstoy, who in 1908 wrote A Letter to a Hindu In it, he declared that the only way for the Indian people could overcome the colonial system was to use the power of love to fight resisting passively. Gandhi was greatly influenced by Tolstoy's theories and the two started the correspondence in 1909 and continued until Tolstoy's passing in the year 1910. [97]

A letter Gandhi sent to Tolstoy in 1910.

Many have said that Gandhism as not only a political ideology, but an economic doctrine social belief system, a religious perspective and perhaps, most importantly a worldview of compassion, all of which are shaped into one. But, upon hearing the word "Gandhism," Gandhi reportedly rejected it: "There is no such concept as 'Gandhism' and I don't want to abandon any sect that is following me. I don't claim to be the originator of any new idea or concept. I simply attempted in my own way to apply timeless truths to our everyday lives and problems...The opinions I've developed and the conclusions I've reached aren't final. I could alter them in the future. I'm not a new person to impart to the world. Truth and nonviolence have been around as long as hills."[98[98]

Yet, Gandhi's ideals of peace, non-violence, and humility have had significant impact on the world over the ages, and continue to influence the world even in the present. Here are a few of the key convictions that are held by Gandhi that must be remembered.

Satyagraha and Swaraj

Satyagraha is often described in the sense of "truth power" also known as "insistence on truth" and the word was invented by Gandhi as a part of his principle of "the power of truth founded on self-suffering and nonviolent courage" as essential to fight for swaraj or freedom. Gandhi identified three key aspects of satyagraha as follows "A constant faith that is rooted in God and the Truth is the most important prerequisite...a Satyagrahi must believe in the triumph of Truth in the saving power and the grace of God...such indefatigable faith alone can make one a person who is able of nonviolence as well as love and forgiveness. Nonviolence, or Ahimsa is the third prerequisite...if the truth is the goal or the goal that is why nonviolence should be the method of achieving it. Tapasya or voluntary suffering can be described as the 3rd quality...tapasya (rigorous mental, physical and moral exercise) improves the inner strength of the spirit."[99[99]

The concept of satyagraha as conceived by Gandhi was implemented in real life through the various non-violent protests he led during his lifetime, both South Africa and India. Gandhi had the firm conviction that in order to bring about liberty and change, you has to be honest, patient and loyal, as well as accepting of one another. The most significant aspect of this belief was Gandhi's notion that in order to effect external changes, such as the structure of the state and independence for the nation as well as changes inside, too and in the form of societal renewal "There is absolutely no impatience, there must be no cruelty and there should be no insolence or unnecessary pressure. If we wish to nurture an authentic democratic spirit, we must not be tolerant. Tolerance is a sign of lack of confidence in one's cause."[100100

For Gandhi to be successful, the fight for Swaraj and political freedom was to be fought together with the wider fight for the rebirth of Indian society. If political independence was the only objective or the most important of the two objectives and if it became the primary goal, then India could be at danger of falling into the same mistakes made by other nations who tried to create a revolutionary government without taking into account the social aspects. The excessive focus on change in the political realm created an environment of careerism where leaders began to look for political advantages and fame over real changes for the benefit of all the people.

The Untouchables

The Dalit or the untouchables as they are also called can be described as (as their name implies) people who are deemed ineligible due to their descent to a caste thought to be impure or less than human.

They do not belong to only one ethnicity or religion however, they are a diverse populace, made up of a range of cultural, religious, linguistic and social classes across India. The Untouchables have been subjected to discrimination due to their perceived impureness and the reasons for the discrimination usually stem from the historical fact that Dalits have been associated with jobs which were considered to be impure in nature, for example, the ones that involve butchering, leatherwork or the removal of animal carcasses as well as garbage. A lot of Dalits employed as butchers cleaning sewers and latrines, or worked in tanneries. Engaging in these kinds of activities was considered as polluting your body and mind and soul of an individual and the resulting pollution was considered to be contagious. The deportation of the untouchables into slums, and the exclusion that was imposed on them to complete involvement in Hindu social activities were a scourge but often overlooked human rights issues in India.

In the year that Gandhi made his first return in India after his return to South Africa in

1915, the Indian leader immediately set out to create an ashram, also known as a spiritual hermitage in Ahmedabad. The issue soon came up of whether he would welcome Dalits to the Satyagraha Ashram: "The Ashram had been operational for only two months before we were put through an examination that I could not have imagined. I received an invitation letter from Amrital Thakkar that reads"An honest, humble family that is not touched by anyone wants to being a part of your Ashram. Do you want to accept the family? I was perturbed...I sent the letter to my friends. They were delighted by it."[101[101

Gandhi therefore welcomed the family members, as that they would respect guidelines of the Ashram. The family's admission to the ashram caused an "flutter" among Gandhi's close friends as well as supporters of the Ashram one of the main worries being that others worried that the public well could be affected and the water would be polluted. Financial support for the ashram ended. In the words of Gandhi, "with the stopping of the monetary aid was the rumor of a social boycott. We were prepared for this. I had informed my fellows that, in the event we were a victim of a boycott and were being denied access to the usual amenities that we wouldn't be leaving Ahmedabad. We'd rather remain in the quarter of the untouchables and eat whatever we could make through manual labor."[102[102

But, financial help came in the form the generous donation of a stranger and the ashram was capable of continuing. Gandhi was able to recall that the financial challenges the ashram faced wasn't the cause of his the greatest anxiety, but that was an "internal turmoil" which he felt as "my senses and eyes were able to detect their (my wife's and my friends') lack of interest or even their disdain" towards Dalits. [103]

The elimination of "untouchability," as Gandhi declared it, was one of his main goals. In 1932 the British government granted the Untouchables distinct electorates under a brand new constitution. It was mostly due to the tireless campaigns of Dalit chief B.R. Ambedkar who was advocating for a separate electoral system similar to the one used in Muslims in India from the early 1900s. This led to untouchables deciding on themselves as their representatives which led to the division of the Dalits into a distinct social and political minority. Gandhi protested against this decision in the belief that the new system of distinct electorates was divisive and even discriminatory, and was a significant obstacle to the unification and common citizenship which Gandhi was fighting for. According to his opinion that the untouchables were integral to Hindu society but having them have the right to vote in a separate way reinforced their status as an independent class, the untouchable and impure class. In more concrete sense, Gandhi knew that a separate electoral system for the Dalits means that he has many fewer supporters.

Gandhi was imprisoned in the year 1898 when the British government refused to listen to his protests and in fact granted separate electorate for the Dalits. Gandhi returned to the old method of protesting; he took a break to protest against an electorate that was separate. Like every other fast, Gandhi's was a major influence on public opinion. Protests were ablaze across the country and forced the government to end the separate electorate, and instead accept the Dalits having seats reserved for them. At this point, Gandhi began calling the untouchables Harijans also known as the children of God and promised to fight for equality and to end the stigma of being untouchable. [104]

Vegetarianism and fasting

A photograph depicts Gandhi praying with Indira Gandhi

His autobiography Gandhi recorded his many struggles with adhering to a vegetarian diet. In his early life and, in particular, while living in London the city, he was pushed to eat meat. But, this experiences were ultimately beneficial to Gandhi because the experience helped him further affirm his convictions about meat consumption. When he was in London, Gandhi came into contact with the movement for vegetarianism in the city and was a part of The London Vegetarian Society. Then, he became a strict vegetarian, particularly after reading the works by Henry Salt, who was an influential advocate for the cause of vegetarianism in London.

For Gandhi to be a vegetarian was not primarily as a matter of health, but as proof, even although he believed that dairy was not vegetarian and avoided it whenever possible, once the doctor told him that his condition could be improved if he consumed dairy products, he began taking goat's milk. So, for Gandhi who was a vegetarian, the choice was about ethics and morals and he stated in a speech he delivered at an event with the London Vegetarian Society in 1931, "I found that a base of selfishness is not a good way of advancing a person higher and higher on the path of evolutionary progress. The only thing that was needed is an altruistic purpose."[105[105] Vegetarianism for Gandhi was more than just diet. It was about self-control, discipline, and the extent to which one willed to fight for one's beliefs and morals.

Gandhi made use of fasting to make a point about politics Since then numerous political activists have utilized the same strategy of hunger strikes and fasting to express their displeasure. His position within Indian society and the worldwide media attention he received contributed to his fasting being an effective weapon. Similar to his diet and decision to celibacy, Gandhi's focus on fasting was much more than just health issues or exercises to improve self-control. In relation to the practice of fasting Gandhi stated, "Fasting...cannot be done by all. A mere physical capacity to perform it is not a requirement for it. It's useless without faith in God. It shouldn't be just a mechanical endeavor or an unjustified limitation. It should come from the core of one's self. This is why it is never easy. There is no room for anger, selfishness or lack of faith anger in a complete fast...Infinite patience, determination and a single-minded focus with a perfect peace of mind, none of the anger needs to be present. Since it is difficult for one to acquire all of these traits at once, anyone who hasn't committed himself to observing the rules of ahimsa ought to undertake the Satyagrahi fast."[106[106]

Fasting was the best method to give up one's body, and to remain in peace. By his fasts Gandhi was a magnet for the media of all kinds as well as changed laws and affected state politics at the highest levels. Fasting was also a way to end massacres and calmed violent violence. In his role as a leader the man has inspired millions of Indians as well as the world to take the way of peace and nonviolence.

Chapter 6: Mahatma Gandhi's Legacy

Mahatma Gandhi

Gandhi with workers from the textile industry in 1931.

Over six decades after the assassination of his father, Gandhi has continued to represent a peace-oriented ideology that has received a cult following and been unparalleled. Gandhi's legacy of non-violence as well as peaceful protest has been invoked numerous times since his death and his views on equality for women, women's rights as well as education and nationalist ideals have shaped the thoughts of many leaders both within and outside of India. In 1937, Gandhi stated during 1937 "My words should be burned alongside my body. The things I've done will last regardless of what I've written or said." written."[107It is certain that the life of his father is most significant legacy and his actions are the most inspiring things he has done. The writer George Orwell noted, "His entire existence was a kind of pilgrimage where every action was significant."[108[108]

However, it's evident that despite all the admiration for Mahatma Gandhi and the acceptance of the superiority of his peace-based principles and nonviolence. Terrorist movements or wars, as well as civil conflicts persist to this day. In India there is a gap in the lives of the rich and the poor is growing in alarming proportions and women's rights are very much unaddressed. Gandhi's stance on celibacy, fasting, and the strictly vegetarian lifestyle has been put controversial and condemned by numerous scholars and research through the years. even Gandhi's followers acknowledged that Gandhi's ideas have been distorted in the minds of people of the present. The Hindu ultranationalists, including one who killed Gandhi continue to thrive as members of the powerful nationalist and right-wing parties.

Prof. Ravinder Kumar, an expert on the life of Gandhi has said that in some ways Gandhi's statements have been neglected after his death, pointing on the ongoing conflicts between the various Indian religions, cultures or ethnic minorities as an excellent instance. Yet one writer has noted, "Most Indians still regard Gandhi and Buddha as one of the greatest characters of Indian history...Gandhi's contribution has been passed on to India is a multi-party democracy that for the vast time is peaceful compared to other Asian nations which are smaller."[109The author of the article says that

In this way Gandhi's name is a legend that has carried for decades even after his death. There is no doubt about his philosophy or doubts regarding how he acted, Mahatma Gandhi and his legacy continues to inspire a lot of people even today and his universal concepts are being embraced by millions of people around the world.

Chapter 7: Who Was Mahatma Gandhi?

Mohandas Karamchand Gandhi was an Indian lawyer as well as an anti-colonial patriot and political ethicist who employed non-violent resistance to lead the victory fight for the country's independence of British rule, and fueled freedom and civil liberties movements across the globe. This epithet Mahtm (which refers to "great-souled" (or "age-old" in Sanskrit) was first given to his name within South Africa in the year 1914, and is used today throughout the world.

Gandhi was born to an Hindu household in seaside Gujarat and then studied in law through The Inner Temple in London.

In 1893, he travelled back to South Africa to represent an Indian businessman in a matter that had been pending for two years in India and could not develop a successful legal practice.

The rest of the two decades of his existence living in South Africa. Gandhi had a family here , and was the first person to employ non-violent protest in the fight for civil liberties.

He returned to India in 1915, when he was at the age of 45. He set out to mobilize farmers, peasants as well as city employees to combat the oppression of land and the high taxes on it. Gandhi directed statewide efforts to combat poverty, promote women's rights, foster friendships between ethnic and spiritual communities as well as eliminate the stigma of untouchability and, most important of all, complete swaraj or self-rule, following the assumption of the management from the Indian National Congress in the year 1921.

Gandhi has contributed greatly to the peace, independence and the culture of India in addition to his non-violent protests that have had a profound impact on the world. Let's look at the other things he did.

Gandhi began wearing a brief dhoti made of hand-spun yarn as a sign of respect of the rural poor in India in 1921. He was living in a self-dependent community and eating only modest meals and being fasting for prolonged durations of time to self-question and political protest. Gandhi encouraged anti-colonial nationalism among ordinary Indians by organizing the 400-kilometer (250-mile) Dandi Salt March in 1930, and also in urging the British to quit India in 1942. Both in South Africa and India, Gandhi was imprisoned several times, and often for lengthy durations of time.

In the beginning of the 1940s Muslim nationalists, who was a proponent of a separate home in the early 1940s for Muslims in British India and weakened Gandhi's ideal that of an independent India founded on spiritual diversity.

Britain granted the independence of India in August 1947. The British Indian Empire was split into two parts, India with a majority

Hindu population and India and Pakistan. Pakistan.

Spiritual violence was evident when displaced Hindus, Muslims, and Sikhs moved to new areas, particularly to Punjab as well as Bengal.

Gandhi examined the affected districts in an effort to lessen the impact of the violence, despite his abstention from main Independence celebrations in Delhi. He participated in numerous hunger strikes during the subsequent months in order to put an end religious violence.

The most recent that began on the 12th of January, 1948, at the time he was 78 served the purpose of encouraging India to give Pakistan some assets of money. Gandhi was perceived by certain Indians for being too friendly towards Pakistan. Nathuram Godse, a Hindu nationalist who killed Gandhi three time in his chest, on the 30th 1948, was one of them.

Young Life and Early Life

Mohandas Karamchand Gandhi was born on October 2nd of 1869 in Porbandar (also known as Sudamapuri) located in the seaside town located on the Kathiawar Peninsula and then part of the handsome and small state of Porbandar within the Indian Empire's Kathiawar Agency. His father, Karamchand Uttamchand Gandhi (from 1822 until 1885) served as the deputy (chief Minister) in the state of Porbandar.

Karamchand proved that he could be a successful chief minister despite having only a basic education. She also worked as a secretary for the State Administration.

Karamchand was married 4 times throughout his time in power. His first two partners died as young men and both after bringing into the world a child. And the third marriage did not produce children. In of 1857 Karamchand requested his third partner to be allowed to remarry and, in the identical year, he got married to Putlibai (from 1844 until 1891) and was who was a

Pranami Vaishnava who was from Junagadh. The next decade was a tumultuous one. Karamchand and Putlibai had three children: a boy, Laxmidas (from around 1860 until 1914) as well as a woman named Raliatbehn (from 1862 until 1960) and a baby, Karsandas (from 1866 to 1913).).

In a drab, unlit ground-floor apartment of the Gandhi family's home in Porbandar city Putlibai conceived her final child, Mohandas, on October 2nd 1869. Gandhi's sister Raliat described the child as "Mercury is a frightened creature who likes to play or frolicking. Doing the ear of dogs was among his favorite actions." The boyhood of Gandhi was influenced with Indian classics, specifically the tales about Shravana as well as King Harishchandra. He writes in his autobiography that they had a lasting impression on him. "It made me feel naive, and I ought to have been Harishchandra in my mind many instances," he writes. The legends of these characters can be traced to Gandhi's self-identification in the early days with love and truth as the most important concepts.

The religious background of the family was diverse. Gandhi's father, Karamchand, was a Hindu and his mother, Putlibai, originated from an Hindu family that was known as Pranami Vaishnavas. Gandhi's father was from the Modh Baniya caste which was part of the Vaishya Varna. His mother came from Pranami, a middle age Krishna Bhakti movement, that was a spiritual force, whose works comprise the Bhagavad Gita and the Bhagavata Purana and fourteen other documents that are based on theories that are believed to contain the core of the Vedas as well as the Quran as well as the Bible.

Gandhi was deeply touched by his mother who was a truly spiritual woman "would never eat food without praying every day ... She took the most difficult vows and adhere to them with no hesitation. For her, fasting 3 or 2 days was nothing at all."

In 1874, Gandhi's father, Karamchand, moved from Porbandar to Rajkot in India, where he became a counsellor of the Thakur Sahib who was the state's ruler. Even though Rajkot was a smaller state than Porbandar however, it was an important home for the British local political organization which was responsible for the security of the diwan of the state.

Karamchand became diwan in Rajkot in 1876. His brother Tulsidas became the successor to Karamchand as diwan in Porbandar in 1877. Following this his return to the family he had left in Rajkot.

Gandhi was enrolled in a small school in Rajkot close to his family at the age of 9 years old. He was introduced to the basics of math as well as the history of Rajkot, Gujarati language, and geography while at the school. He enrolled in Alfred High School in Rajkot at the age of eleven years old. He was a normal student who was awarded a few prizes however, the timid and tongue-tied child who didn't have a lot of interest in sports; his only true acquaintances were schoolbooks and courses.

In May 1883 Mohandas Gandhi, at thirteen years old, was married Kasturbai Makhanji Kapadia at the time she was 14 years old (her name was changed in the name to "Kasturba," and passionately to "Bachelor's degree") in an arrangement marriage according to the tradition in the region in the time.

He missed a whole year of school due to this, but it was later permitted to make up the missed time through speeding up his studies. The wedding ceremony was a celebration of the family, with his brother and his cousin being married as well. "As we did not know much about weddings, to us it was just about wearing new clothes and eating sweet foods and spending time with family and friends," he once specified of their wedding. The bride-to-be-to-be in her teens was expected to spend lots spent with family members as well as from her spouse in the traditional way.

"Even at school , I used to think of her and the thought of dark and the subsequent meeting was always a constant worry for my mind," Mohandas wrote several years later, regretting his sexual desire for his future bride. He later admitted to being insecure and jealous of her, particularly when she was going to an temple with her buddies and that his feelings toward her was sexually intense.

The father of Gandhi, Karamchand, passed away in the latter part of 1885.

Gandhi was 16 years old at the time as well as his 17-year-old wife had their first child, who lived only a few days. Gandhi was devastated by the two deaths. Harilal was born in 1888. Manilal was born around 1892. Ramdas birthed in 1897 and Devdas born in 1900 were the Gandhi family's other four sons.

Gandhi aged 18 years old, graduated from the high school in Ahmedabad in November 1887.

He enrolled in Samaldas College in Bhavnagar State in January 1888. It was the only degree-granting institution in the nineties. But he left and returned to Porbandar to spend time with his family.

Gandhi was the only inexpensive college of Bombay that was affordable for him to pay for.

The Gandhi family was persuaded through Mavji Dave Joshiji Mavji Dave Joshiji, Mavji Dave Joshiji, a Brahmin Priest and family friend to pursue legal education in London.

His companion Kasturba was the one to bring to life their first child of enduring, Harilal, in the month of July 1888.

Gandhi's mother rebuked him for to stay with his family and friends and traveling away from home. Tulsidas his uncle, who was Gandhi's, tried to persuade his nephew. Gandhi wanted to leave. Gandhi made a promise in front of his mother to avoid eating meat or red wine as well as women to encourage his girlfriend as well as his mother. Gandhi's brother Laxmidas who was an attorney was elated Gandhi on his plans to pursue a degree and study in London and offered his assistance to him. Gandhi was granted the authority of Putlibai, and his true blessing.

Gandhi was then just 18 years old Gandhi, who was then just 18 years old, left Porbandar to head for Mumbai which was then called Bombay on the 10th of August in 1888. He was a member of the local Modh Bania community upon his arrival. There, the senior members advised him to beware that England might lure the man to abandon his faith by drinking and eating according to Western methods. Gandhi was thrown out of his tribe despite notifying them of his commitment to his mother and her genuine blessings. Gandhi didn't care and made the decision to travel through Bombay in India to London on the 4th of September and was joined by his brother. Gandhi was studying of University College, London, which is part of the University of London.

He was a student of the law and jurisprudence of UCL and was admitted to the Inner Temple to chase after the career of lawyer. The shyness and self-detachment he experienced in his young age lasted through the teenage years. When he moved to London and stayed with the same traits, but he enrolled in a group of public speaking instructors and overcome his shyness to be able to practice law.

He expressed his deep concern about the health of the dockland population in London's poorest condition. A major trade war broke out in London in 1889. Dockers were striking to get better wages and working conditions, as well as shipbuilders, seafarers, factory workers, and other taking part in a uniform. The strikers won because of Cardinal Manning's mediation. This prompted Gandhi along with an Indian good friend to give the strikers a check and express gratitude to thank him for the efforts.

Indian Independence Struggle Indian Independence Struggle

Gandhi returned to India in 1915 on the advice by Gopal Krishna Gokhale who was passed on to Gandhi from C. F. Andrews. He was an eminent Indian nationalism, theorist as well as a community leader, Gandhi earned an international reputation.

Gokhale was Gandhi's first introduction to Indian issues political issues, the Indian system, along with the Indian people after Gokhale joined the Indian National Congress. Gokhale was a prominent participant within the Congress Party who was acknowledged for his diligence and modest sums, as well as his commitment to the political system. Gandhi modified Gokhale's liberal approach that was based on British Whiggish practices in order to make it appear Indian.

In 1920 Gandhi took over the leadership of Congress and began increasing the needs until that the Indian National Congress announced India's independence on January 26 in 1930.

The British didn't accept the statement however, settlements were continued and in the latter part of the 1930s in the 1930s, the Congress was appointed a position in the provincial federal government. In 1939, when the Viceroy declared the war against Germany without any assessment during September, 1939 Gandhi along with the Congress ended their support for the Raj.

The stress grew to the point where in 1942 Gandhi wanted to declare independence immediately, which led the British to imprison him as well as 10s of thousands of Congress leaders. The Muslim League worked together with Britain and pushed for a distinct Muslim state in Pakistan despite Gandhi's strong opposition.

The British divided the terrain during July 1947. and with India and Pakistan becoming independent under conditions Gandhi disliked.

His role in WW1

In the last days during World War I, the Viceroy of India invited Gandhi to the War Conference in Delhi in April 1918.

Gandhi has promised to aid in the efforts of the war by hiring Indians.

In contrast to those who participated in the Zulu War of 1906 and the start of The First World War in 1914 the year 1914, when Gandhi sought volunteers to join The Ambulance Corps, this time Gandhi sought out candidates.

In a booklet that was released during the June of 1918, it was titled ""

To create such a condition of affairs, we must be able to protect ourselves, i.e. the ability to carry weapons and utilize weapons," Gandhi mentioned in his "Application for Enlistment." The army is the only way to go in order to master how to utilize weapons at the fastest speed possible."

In a letter addressed to the viceroy's personal secretary the Viceroy did say, however, that the Viceroy "personally will not hurt or kill anyone whether a good friend or foe."

Gandhi's nonviolence has been questioned on by his war participation project. "The issue of coherence between his 'Ahimsa' creed (nonviolence) as well as his war enrollment project was not just raised in the past, but also ever since," Gandhi's personal secretary wrote.

In 1917, Gandhi's initial significant accomplishment was the Champaran protests in Bihar.

The Champaran protests pitted local people against their mostly British owners and were backed by the city's government.

The peasants were instructed to cultivate Indigofera as a crop of money to Indigo color that was escalating for more than twenty yearsof drought, and then to sell their produce to planters at the cost of a fixed amount.

The peasantry, unhappy with this, gathered to petition Gandhi at his Ashram in Ahmedabad. Gandhi's peaceful demonstration technique was a surprise to the regulars and caused concessions from authorities.

Kheda was affected by the effects of floods and scarcity in 1918. The peasantry demanded relief from taxes.

Gandhi relocated his office to Nadiad with the assistance of many supporters and new volunteers from the region, one of the most important is Vallabhbhai Patel.

Gandhi initiated the signature drive by that used non-cooperation as a strategy that required peasants to pledge not to pay homage the threat of confiscation of their land.

The protest was accompanied with a protest by mamlatdars as well as talatdars (district profit authorities). Gandhi was determined to win popular support for his struggle.

The government was able to withstand for 5 months however by the end of May 1918 it was clear that the government of the United States had retreated on the most important provisions and had reduced the tax on earnings until the war was over.

Vallabhbhai Patel represented the farmers in Kheda during settlements with British who stopped their revenue collection and released all inmates.

The Khilafat Movement

After World War I, Gandhi (then aged 49) was looking for Muslim political backing in his struggle against British imperialism, by defending the Ottoman Empire which was defeated in the conflict.

The common squabbles and riots among Hindus and Muslims were prevalent during the time of British India just before Gandhi's initiative, much like the riots from 1917 until 18. Gandhi had already assisted the British monarchy in terms of economics and also by bringing in Indian warriors to join them during the European conflict.

Gandhi's efforts were bolstered partly by the British promise to repay Indians for their assistance in Swaraj (self-government) when World War 1 ended.

Instead of self-government, the British federal government instead offered Gandhi minor changes, which he refused to down. Gandhi declared his intention to participate in the satyagraha (civil non-violence). In the year 1896, the Rowlatt Act was gone by

British colonial authorities as an alternative to Gandhi's protests.

The Act gave that the British federal government with the legal authority to prosecute those who are lawbreakers, and to hold anyone to "preventive indefinite detention or imprisonment without judicial review or the requirement of the possibility of trial."

Gandhi believed that cooperation among Hindus as well as Muslims was crucial to advancement of the cause to fight the British. He was a major proponent out of this Khilafat movement, which Sunni Muslims in India, with the help of sultans of Baronial States in India as well as Ali brothers Ali brothers, supported an official title of Turkish Caliph as an example to show Sunni Islamic unity (ummah).

Following that the Ottoman Empire was defeated during World War I, they believed that the Caliph was an option to defend Islam and Islamic law.

The Khilafat movement gained Gandhi's support, but the results were not equally. This resulted in a huge Muslim backing for Gandhi from the beginning.

Hindu leaders, including Rabindranath Tagore, challenged Gandhi's leadership simply because they did not want being against the Sunni Islamic Caliph of Turkey being recognized or backed.

The increase in Muslim sympathy for Gandhi as he pushed the cause of the Caliph for a short time, ended the violent conflict among Hindus as well as Muslims.

In the combined Rowlatt the satyagraha-related parades it proved the community unity and increased Gandhi's stature as an official to the British.

Muhammad Ali Jinnah, who declared his opposition to Gandhi's non-cooperation technique, satyagraha and was boosted by his support of Khilafat. Khilafat project. Jinnah began to build his own network of support and eventually became the main force behind the need for a distinct West as well as East Pakistan.

While they agreed on the main goal of Indian independence but they were unable to agree on the best way to get there. Instead of trying to rally people, Jinnah was able to negotiate with British by negotiating constitutional amendments.

Khilafat movement was defeated. Khilafat group was deposed by the end of 1922.

Turkey's Ataturk had brought his stamp on the caliphate as well as the Khilafat movement and Muslim backing for Gandhi. Gandhi's Congress was rebuked from the throne of Muslim leaders and the delegates. Conflicts among Hindus and Muslims have returned. Religious riots have been reported in a few locations, with 91 deaths reported from Agra and Oudh in the United Provinces of Agra and Oudh in the United Provinces of Agra.

Unhappy to collaborate

Gandhi who was then 40 years old of age, wrote in the book Hind Swaraj (which was in 1909) that British rule in India was established through the help of Indians and has lasted solely because of this cooperation. British rule would end in the event that Indians were not willing to cooperate and Swaraj (Indian freedom) would be the next step.

Gandhi informed his Viceroy India via telegraph in February 1919 warning him that if British adopted the Rowlatt Act, he would draw Indians to begin civil protests.

It was the British federal government ignored his wishes and passed the law and announced that it would not be frightened. There were many protesters who gathered to protest to the Rowlatt Act, leading to the satyagraha civil dissent. On the 30th March 1919 British officers opened firing on a unarmed group of protesters peacefully gathering in Delhi to participate in the Satyagraha.

In retaliation, people rioted. He advised a crowd on the sixth of April, 1919 which was which was a Hindu festival day to avoid hurt or cause harm to British citizens, but rather to express their anger in peace by banning British products and burning all British clothes they owned. Even if one faction used violence in the event, he emphasized the principle of nonviolence in the face of the British and each other. People across India have indicated their intention to oppose in larger number. Gandhi was ordered from the Federal government to not visit Delhi. Gandhi did not heed the order. Gandhi was arrested on the 9th of April.

There was an unrest. On the 13th of April, 1919 the British officer named Reginald Dyer surrounded a group of people at Amritsar park. Amritsar park, which included but not only girls and women and ordered his soldiers to open fire on the group.

The infamous Jallianwala Bagh massacre (or Amritsar massacre) of several Sikh and Hindu citizens infuriated the subcontinent, yet was celebrated by some Britons and a portion in some of the British press as being a need-to response. Gandhi did not slam for the British in Ahmedabad following the savage slaughter in Amritsar rather, he was criticized by his fellow citizens for not using only love to combat those who support the British federal government's hate. Gandhi was the one to call for the end of the violence and destruction of property and also went on an execution fast to force Indians to stop the riots.

Many people were shocked by the murders and Gandhi's nonviolent response and certain Sikhs and Hindus were furious over the fact that Dyer got free of murder. The British established investigations committees that Gandhi suggested Indians to avoid. The events of that day, which included the massacre as well as the British response, convinced Gandhi that Indians were never treated in the same manner under British rule. Gandhi switched his focus on swaraj as well as the establishment of a political independent for India. Gandhi was the leader of the Indian National Congress during the year 1921. He was the one who reorganized Congress. Gandhi enjoyed the political backing and the interest that was expected from those in the British Raj, thanks to the backing from Congress in addition to Muslim support that was triggered through his backing for his support for the Khilafat project to reinstate his position as the Caliph within Turkey.

Gandhi's non-violent non-cooperation platform was expanded in order to incorporate the Swadeshi rule which is a boycott of foreign-made items, particularly British products. The demand that to all Indians to wear Khadi (homemade fabric) instead of British-made fabric was linked to this.

Gandhi advised Indian both men and women rich and poor to gather around spinning daily to support fight for liberty. Gandhi demanded that people avoid British organisations and courts, quit federal government positions and refuse British titles and honours as well as abstaining from British products. This was the reason Gandhi's journey began to politically, financially, and administratively imprison and destabilize the British India government.

The idea of "non-cooperation" emerged and its reputation in the social sphere attracted people from all walks of life across India. On the 10th of March 1922 Gandhi had been arrested and accused of sedition and sentenced to six years of jail.

On the 18th March, 1922, he began his sentence. After Gandhi was imprisoned in 1922, the Indian National Congress divided into two factions: one that was led by Chitta Ranjan Das and Motilal Nehru who advocated participation of the party in legislatures, and the other, led by Chakravarti Rajagopalachari as well as Sardar Vallabhbhai Patel, who opposed the idea. Furthermore as the Khilafat movement fell apart with the ascendance of Ataturk in

Turkey The co-operation among Hindus and Muslims ended. Muslim leaders broke off of the Congress and established Muslim businesses. Gandhi's political base split into various groups. Gandhi got released February 1924 following only two years of imprisonment in the wake of an appendix procedure.

The Famous Salt March

Gandhi continued to pursue swaraj during the second half of 1920s following his release from prison for political infractions at the time of 1924. On December 28, 1928 he tried to push through a resolution in the Calcutta Congress demanding that the British federal government grant India ruling status or else face an entirely new plan of non-cooperation with the aim of achieving complete independence for the country. Some, such as Subhas Chandra Bose as well as Bhagat Singh, had doubts about his morals and nonviolent methods following his position of support to The First World War with Indian battle troops and the inability to the Khilafat movement in preserving the Caliph's rule in Turkey and the decline of Muslim acceptance of his administration.

Although numerous Hindu leaders pushed for immediate freedom, Gandhi minimized his need to hold off for a one-year period instead of two years.

Gandhi's ideas weren't received well in the British. In talks with European diplomats who were tolerant of Indian requests, British political leaders like as Lord Birkenhead and Winston Churchill announced their animosity towards "the people who favored Gandhi." In Lahore there was an Indian flag was raised December 31st 29th, 1929. On the day of India's Independence Day, January twenty-sixth 30th, 1930 Gandhi was the leader of Congress in an celebration in Lahore. Every Indian business celebrated this day. In the month of March, 1930 Gandhi started a second Satyagraha to protest taxation by the British salt tax. On March 2, Gandhi released a warning in the form of a personal letter addressed to Lord Irwin Viceroy of

India. The letter Gandhi declared British rule as a "curse" and said it "has been able to squander the pennies of millions through an oppression system that is progressive and a horribly expensive civil administration and army ... It has reduced us into a state of serfdom." The letter Gandhi further stated that the viceroy's salary was "practically five thousand times India's normal salary." Gandhi has also stressed his determination to peaceful methods of protest within the document.

It was the Salt March to Dandi, that took place from March 12 through April 6 was a major highlight of this, as Gandhi marched for 388 km (241 miles) from Ahmedabad to Dandi, Gujarat, with more than 78 participants with the specific goal of breaking the salt law. The 240-mile journey took Gandhi 25 days to complete which included Gandhi giving speeches to huge crowds on the way. In Dandi his home town, he was joined by the 10s of thousands of Indians. On May 5th the accused was arrested by a decree of 1827 ahead of a planned presentation. On the 21st of May He was not during the Dharasana salt plant's demonstration. Webb Miller, an annoyed American reporter, summarized the British reaction in the following manner:

"The Gandhi men prepared and were stopped just at a distance of one hundred yards away from the stockade in silence. In the crowd, an unorganized column advancing, explored the ditches and eventually reached the barbed wire fence. ... upon a shout the native police attacked the marchers, pouring bamboo sticks made of steel shot down onto their heads. There was not a single marcher who moved his arm to block the strikes. They fell like ninepins. The terrible thud of clubs hitting heads that were exposed could be heard from where I was ... The victims were hit were normal, sprawled or unconscious, or wriggling, saw their shoulders or skulls were fractured."

The march lasted for several hours, until at the minimum, three hundred demonstrators were hit, many of them seriously injured and 2 of them were killed. They didn't stage any sort of resistance.

This was among his most reliable initiatives in sabotaging the British control of India The British reacting by placing into prison nearly 60,000 of the Indian population.

Estimates from Congress however, on contrary estimate the total at 90,000. Jawaharlal Nehru was among them. He was also one Gandhi's lieutenants was one of the others.

Gandhi as per Sarma employed women to be part of salt tax initiatives and boycotts of foreign goods which gave women a renewed self-confidence and self-esteem within Indian society.

Others, such as Marilyn French, claim that Gandhi barred women from participating in the civil disobedience protests due to fear of being accused in the use of women as a security force for his political stance. If women wanted to sign up for the project and taking part in rallies held on public occasions, Gandhi advised the volunteers to obtain permission from their guardians, and to only be a part of the movement if they could provide childcare. In spite of Gandhi's concerns and opinions, many Indian women participated in the Salt March to oppose British salt prices and the monopoly of salt mining. Women marched and protested against stores independently following Gandhi's detention, and endured a plethora of attacks and abuse verbally from British officials in Gandhi's spirit. Gandhi.

Negotiating

In the 1920s The Indian Congress used Telugu language plays to attract Andhra Pradesh peasants, integrating Indian legends and folklore into Gandhi's beliefs and presenting Gandhi as a savior and a reincarnation for the age-old and middle-age Indian nationalist saints and heroes.

According to Murali his plays won popularity with the people who lived in traditional Hindu culture. Gandhi was subsequently the most popular hero of Telugu-speaking communities, a revered and revered messiah character.

The views of Gandhi, as per Dennis Dalton, was accountable to his widespread appeal. Gandhi condemned Western civilization as a result of being based on "strength and morality" contrary to his definition of Indian society as being based on "soul morality and force." Gandhi's views on beating "hatred by loving" fascinated the creative the people who influenced his fathers. These views can be found in his works from the 1890s. They were widely known to Indian working indentured from South Africa. People gathered around him upon his return to India just because he displayed their idealistic views.

Gandhi also put forth a joint effort to promote his message in the backwoods throughout all of the Indian subcontinent.

He used terms and phrases from the Ramayana including Rama-rajya, Prahlada as iconic icons as well as cultural symbols, such as another component of swaraj as well as satyagraha. Beyond India the beliefs of these people were not prevalent throughout his life but they were quickly and psychologically connected with the society of his time and values from the past.

Lord Irwin Lord Irwin, who represented his federal counterpart, opted to join forces with Gandhi. In the month of March 1931, Gandhi as well as Irwin were the first to sign the Gandhi-Irwin Pact. Irwin Pact. For the purpose of extending the civil disobedience protest in 1931, the British federal government agreed to release all political prisoners. Gandhi was invited to attend the Round Table Conference in London for discussions and was also the sole representative of the Indian National Congress, according to the treaty. Gandhi along with the Nationalists, were unhappy with the gathering. Gandhi wanted to speak about India's independence, however

India's British part was far more concerned with Indian minorities and princes rather than a transfer of power. Lord Willingdon Lord Irwin's heir who was Lord Irwin's heir, stood firm against India as a nation that was independent and began a new campaign to thwart and stop the nationalism movement. Gandhi was arrested again and authorities tried but were unable to neutralize his influence by segregating his supporters from him.

Winston Churchill, a popular Conservative politician who was clearly out of his post at the time, but was later elected the first Prime and Minister in the U.K., ended up being a ferocious and important criticism of Gandhi and a major opponent of his long-standing objectives throughout the UK. Gandhi was frequently mocked by Churchill who, in a widely distributed 1931 speech that,

" It's shocking and horrifying to watch Mr. Gandhi as known as a seditious Middle Temple legal representative, suddenly acting as a fakir, a kind that is well-known in the East walking half-naked on the steps of the Vice-regal palace ... in order to negotiate in a manner that is on par with the King's emissary." Emperor's.

Through the 30s and 40s Churchill's resentment toward Gandhi intensified. Gandhi was, as he claimed was "seditious in the sense of intent," with wickedness and multiform risk that targeted an entire British empire. He was labeled an "Hindu Mussolini" by Churchill for provoking the racial conflict and attempting to alter the Raj through Brahmin friends, and praising the ignorance of the Indian people, all to gain personal gain. Churchill tried to break the ties between Gandhi from his criticism of Gandhi was often portrayed through European and American newspapers. This won Churchill's approval however, it also helped Gandhi's popularity among Europeans. Churchill made it clear to the "British themselves could be deprived of peace and a misdirected conscience" because of the changes.

In The Round Table conferences that took place between Gandhi with government officials of the British federal government during 1931 and 32, Gandhi, now around 60 years old was looking for constitutional reforms as a prelude to the end of colonial British government and the beginning of Indian autonomy.

The British sought to find ways to ensure the Indian subcontinent's recognition as a unit. The British mediators proposed constitutional reforms based on their British Rule model, which divided electorates according to classes and religious departments. The British challenged Gandhi's credibility to spread his message across India as well as his support for the Congress party. They called Indian spiritual leaders, such as Muslims and Sikhs as well as B. R. Ambedkar as their representative leader, in order to stimulate their spiritual needs. Gandhi was strongly opposed to any constitution that codified the rights of agents or rights in common departments, claiming that it would create division instead of uniting the people and perpetuate their status and distract attention from the efforts of India to end settlement control.

Between 1914 and 1948, he departed India to attend his second Round Table conference. He turned down the federal government's offer to the possibility of a room in a stylish West End hotel, deciding instead to stay within the East End and live amongst the class of the poor, like he did in India. In the three months of his stay and stay, he was in a small cell-room in Kingsley Hall, where he was welcomed to East Enders. He was reconnected to those who were part of the British vegetarian movement at this time.

Gandhi started a new satyagraha upon returning after his participation in the 2nd Round Table Conference. He was snatched and placed into the Pune's Yerwada Prison. In the time he was in jail it was his British federal government enacted an amendment that gave people who are not able to vote their own electorate. The award was known as"the Communal Award. In prison, Gandhi started a fast-unto-death in a form of protest. A subsequent public outrage forced on the government of the United States to alter its Communal Award with the Poona Pact which was developed together with Ambedkar.

Politics in Congress

Gandhi quit his position in the Congress party in 1934. He did not disagree with the position of the party, but the truth was that should he leave in 1934, his appeal to Indians could no longer be a hindrance to the Congress party's membership, which included socialists, communists, students, trade unionists spiritual conservatives, as well as people who had pro-business beliefs and that all the voices of these groups would get an opportunity of being heard. In presenting a celebration of those who was able to accept a temporary political compromise to Gandhi's Raj, Gandhi wanted to avoid becoming the target of Raj propaganda.

Under Nehru's presidency, and during his Congress's Lucknow session in 1936 Gandhi was back in active politics. Despite Gandhi's wishes to get the Congress to be centered on the task of achieving independence, not making predictions about the future of India and its future, the Congress took socialism as its goal. Subhas Chandra Bose, who was chosen as to be the president in 1938, and who had previously expressed reservations about nonviolence as a method of protest and reacted to Gandhi. Even though Gandhi was opposed, Bose beat Gandhi's choice Doc. Pattabhi Sitaramayya for another period as Congress President. However, Bose resigned from the party when the All-India leaders resigned in large in protest at his disapproval of Gandhi's ideas. Sitaramayya's loss, Gandhi claimed was his defeat.

The Quit India movement and the Second World War

Gandhi was adamant against any Indian involvement in the second world conflict and also against any assistance to the British efforts to fight.

Gandhi's plan failed because it didn't have the backing of the Indian population and several Indian leaders such as but not only Sardar Patel as well as Rajendra Prasad. More than 2.5 million Indians were able to defy Gandhi and joined the British Armed Force to fight alongside the allies on across a variety of fronts.

Gandhi's criticism of India's involvement during the Second World War stemmed from the view that India was not an occasion to celebrate an apparent war fought for democratic freedom even if India itself was not allowed this freedom.

He also criticized Nazism as well as Fascism which was a position that was shared by many others Indian leaders. Gandhi's call for independence grew stronger as war raged on which culminated with a speech in 1942 in Mumbai in which he demanded that the British quit India. This was Gandhi's as well as the Congress Party's most decisive rebellion, with the goal of forcing the British to leave India. The British authorities reacted immediately at Gandhi's Quit India address, apprehending Gandhi as well as all members of the Congress Working Committee within hours of the speech. A number of train stations that were owned by the government as well as police headquarters as well as telegraph cable cables, were damaged or destroyed in response to the detentions.

Gandhi who was nearing the age of 70 at the time and advised his followers to stop obeying the royal authority in 1942. In this regard he advised people not to murder or injure British residents however, he advised them to be willing to be a victim and die should British authorities begin to take taking action. He emphasized that the movement could not be stopped as an outcome of violence committed by individuals by stating that "the current administration's" "regulated the anarchy" was "even more dangerous than actual anarchy." As a reason of their right to rights and liberties he encouraged Indians into Karo"ya Maro" ("do and die").

Gandhi was detained in Gandhi was detained in the Aga Khan Palace of Pune for two years during his time in detention. In this period his long-serving secretary Mahadev Desai died of an cardiac arrest. His partner Kasturba died on February 22 1944, following 18 months in prison, and Gandhi was struck by a severe malaria attack. He agreed for an interview Stuart Gelder, a British reporter, while incarcerated. Gelder then wrote and published an account of the interview that he sent to the mainstream press, showing Gandhi's newfound willingness to compromise and words that astonished his followers, Congress workers, and even Gandhi. The second and third parties claimed they misrepresented Gandhi's actual remarks on a variety of topics and wrongly condemning his Quit India movement.

Due to his declining health and the necessity for surgical intervention, Gandhi was released before the war ended on May 6th 1944. The Raj did not want him to spend the rest of his life in prison and irritate the populace. Gandhi was released from jail to an evolving political scene: there was a new political landscape: the Muslim League, which had been tiny a few years earlier, "now controlled the center of the political arena" and Muhammad Ali Jinnah's campaign to establish Pakistan was a hot topic. Gandhi and Jinnah were in constant contact and the two men had numerous meetings over two weeks in September 1944. during which Gandhi was pushing for a unified continuous plural, independent India that included Muslims and non-Muslims collaborating. The plan was rejected by Jinnah who insisted on dividing the subcontinent according to spiritual boundaries to create a distinct Muslim India (later Pakistan).

The discussions continued to last until 1947. When the top Congress's leaders Congress were detained and the other parties gathered to support the war and grew in size. Congress was relentless in its repression of publications that were underground, even though it was unable to influence things. The British provided clear indications that they would hand over control to Indian hands after the conclusion of the conflict. In the midst of this, Gandhi declared a halt to the fight, and more than 100,000 political prisoners comprising the Congress management was released.

Gandhi was an outspoken critic of the division of the spiritual world in India's Indian subcontinent.

Gandhi and Gandhi and the Indian National Congress promoted for the British to quit India. They also urged the Muslim League, on the contrary, demanded for India be divided and be left to its own.

Gandhi proposed a method by in which would see the Congress along with the Muslim League could negotiate in order to gain independence under a provisional administration. Following that, the question to partition was decided through a plebiscite within Muslim-majority districts.

Jinnah did not agree with Gandhi's proposal and demanded the establishment of a Direct Action Day on August 16th, 1946. This was to gather Muslims in cities to back his plan to separate India. Indian subcontinent in Muslim States and states that were not Muslim. The Calcutta authorities were granted the opportunity to enjoy a special holiday to mark Direct Action Day by Huseyn Shaheed Suhrawardy, who was the Muslim League Chief Minister of Bengal which is today Bangladesh in Bangladesh and West Bengal. Calcutta Hindus were massacred in a mass shooting and their properties were burnt due to the Direct-Action Day, and holidaying officers were not able to stop the violence. In the end, the British federal government did not send warriors out to quell the rage. Violence that was vindictive against Muslims was a common occurrence all over India due to the violence of Direct Action Day. The following days many Hindus or Muslims were killed and hundreds of thousands were injured in a vicious cycle of violence. Gandhi went into the districts that had the highest rate of riots in order to demand an end to these violence.

Before and after granting Indian independence as a concept, Archibald Wavell, the Governor-General and Viceroy in British India for 3 years from February 1947 to February 1947, worked against Gandhi and Jinnah in search of an agreement. Gandhi's character, his intentions and views were all attacked by Wavell. Gandhi was described as an "deadly brutal, vicious, and incredibly clever" politician by Wavell and accused Gandhi as having a singular purpose in "conquering British control and impact and establishing the concept of a Hindu Raj." Wavell was worried about a civil war threatening the Indian subcontinent and doubted Gandhi's ability to end the conflict.

The British were reluctant to grant the Indian subcontinent's population to have freedom and freedom, but they also agreed with Jinnah's plan to divide the region in Pakistan in the two countries of India.

Gandhi was in India in the last settlements however, in the words of Stanley Wolpert, Gandhi "never ever endorsed or approved the idea of separating British India."

The split was highly contested and strongly objected to. More than 500,000 were killed in riots of spirituality during the time that countless people who were not Muslims (generally Hindus and Sikhs) fled from Pakistan towards India and Muslims were forced to move away from India to Pakistan across the recently established boundaries that were recently established between India, West Pakistan, and East Pakistan.

On the 15th of August, 1947 Gandhi was able to spend his Independence Day with a fast and spinning in Calcutta but not celebrating the ending of British rule, but instead hoping for peace among the people he shared a common ground with. The Indian subcontinent was covered in spiritual warfare since partition, and streets were filled with bodies. Gandhi's protests and fasting have been credited by some authors as having put an end to religious riots and violence.

Gandhi was assassinated

Gandhi was seen with his grandnieces on the Birla Home premises Birla House (now Gandhi Smriti) at 5:17 p.m. on the 30th, 1948, on his way to attend an assembly of prayer at which point Hindu Nationalist Nathuram Godse shot 3 bullets into his chest with an assault rifle in close proximity. Gandhi was believed to have died immediately as per accounts.

Gandhi was taken to his home, the Birla Home, and was placed in the bed room according to various reports, similar to one published by an eyewitness journalist. He died about thirty minutes later, as the family members of Gandhi was reading Hindu scriptures.

Then, on All-India Radio, Prime Minister Jawaharlal Nehru addressed his countrymen by saying:

"Good family and friends Our light in our lives is headed out and darkness is everywhere and I'm not sure of how to express myself or show the darkness. Our beloved Leader, Bapu, the dad of our country has left us. It's possible that I'm wrong but we will not see Bapu as often as we have been for so many years. And we will not seek help or comfort from him, which is a devastating loss, not just to me, but for millions of others across this country."

Godse was a Hindu nationalist who was a part of Mahasabha, the Hindu Mahasabha, didn't make any effort to flee along with other conspirators. They were arrested shortly after.

They were trialed before Delhi's Red Fort of Delhi. Godse did not deny the allegations or express remorse during his trial. As per Claude Markovits, a French chronicler renowned for his on colonial India, Godse mentioned that Godse killed Gandhi because of his indifference toward Muslims He held Gandhi responsible for his bloodshed as well as the the suffering that occurred at the time of partition of India's subcontinent between Pakistan in the year 1947 and India.

Gandhi was accused in the eyes of Godse of subjectivism, and believing that he had an absolute authority over truth. In 1949 Godse had been convicted of and killed.

The death of Gandhi was mourned by many. Nearly a million people took part in the funeral procession that lasted five miles starting from Birla Home, where he was murdered at the time, towards Raj Ghat, which took five hours for the police to arrive. an additional hundred thousand watched it pass through. Gandhi's body was transported onto a weapons supplier and the vehicle's chassis was taken away overnight to allow the setting up of a high-floor so that the public could view his body. The engine of the car was not used as a substitute for drag-ropes each manned by 50 people, were used to drag the vehicle. The majority of Indian-owned businesses in

London were closed as thousands of people from all religious and denominational backgrounds as well as Indians from across the country were gathered at the India Home in London.

The death of Mahatma Gandhi revolutionized the political landscape for ever and for ever. His successor in power was Nehru. According to Markovits the statement of Pakistan that it was an "Muslim state" caused Indian organizations to request to make it as a "Hindu state" even though Gandhi was alive. Nehru made Gandhi's death an instrument of political power to silence the majority of Hindu nationalism supporters and opponents to his political agenda. He linked Gandhi's murder to hatred and ill-will politics.

Nehru as well as his Congress coworkers, as per Guha, inspired Indians to pay tribute to Gandhi's memory and, most importantly his ideas.

Nehru made use of the assassination in order to boost the newly formed Indian state's power. The large number of Hindu expressions of discontent with an individual who had been influential to them for decades was a way to boost the public's support for the federal government, and also legitimize the control of Congress Party. With the arrest of 200,000 in the first week, the federal government was able to repress those who were part of the RSS, Muslim National Guards and Khaksars.

"Gandhi's shadow was omnipresent throughout the political landscape of the newly formed Indian Republic for several years following his assassination." says Markovits. In reviving Gandhi's ideas and image the federal government was able to have the power to limit any criticisms to its social and financial policies regardless of the fact they did not conform to Gandhi's views.

In accordance with Hindu tradition, Gandhi was cremated. The ashes of Gandhi were placed into urns and sent to India to commemorate his life. The 12th of February 1948, a lot of the ashes were placed in the Sangam in Allahabad However, certain ashes were removed in a discreet manner. Tushar Gandhi dumped into the contents of an urn that was found in a safe deposit box, and restored by the courts, to the Sangam in Allahabad in 1997. Gandhi's ashes were scattered in the vicinity of Jinja, Uganda, near the source of the Nile River, along with a monument is dedicated to the event. Another urn's contents were submerged in Girgaum Chowpatty on the 30th of January in 2008. Another urn is found in the Aga Khan's residence located in Pune (where Gandhi was sent to prison as a political detainee between 1942 until 1944) as well as the Self-Realization Fellowship Lake Shrine in Los Angeles.

The location of Gandhi's assassination, Birla Home, is today a memorial site known by the name of Gandhi Smriti. It is the Rj Ght memorial in New Delhi near the Yamuna

River, is where the body of Gandhi was buried.

Chapter 8: What Was The Reason The Mahatma His Name? Mahatma?

Mahatma simply means "Great Soul" or revered and respected. - - and Gandhi was definitely an outstanding soul, without doubt. The title was bestowed his name in the year 1914 in recognition of his unwavering fight against oppression and discrimination of the weak through the power of. There is also a legend Gurudev RabindranathTagore bestowed the title "Mahatma" for Gandhi.

While different sources offer various details about when and who the title was conferred to M.K. Gandhi There is no doubt about the reason the title was bestowed to M.K. Gandhi. It was because of the compassion that he displayed for others as well as his unbeatable fight spirit simple way of life, and his ability to inspire people to stand up and struggle for the rights of others in a peaceful manner.

Why did he get the name Bapu?

"Bapu" is a different word for father in many Indian languages. He was the father figure of all. While India was a single nation as an British colony however, it was divided in terms of culture and socially, but he was able to bring the country together under his impartial and competent direction. Gandhi was known as Bapu by many to show gratitude and respect they felt for the man inside their souls.

He was the most adored leader of the struggling Indian people, and millions of Indians were able to see as a father figure who would lead them away from their oppression by British Empire. British Empire.

Later on, he was called the 'Father of the Nation'. In accordance with the title given to Gandhi, Gandhi had love and compassion for all Indians like fathers should have regard for their children. He did not discriminate against them because of their status or caste.

Gandhi creating his own fabric on a "charkha"

What exactly is Ahimsa?

Gandhi was a champion of Ahimsa which in Sanskrit means to not cause anyone, inflict pain or cause harm to anyone or anything. It's a way of life that is non-violence throughout every aspect of life, regardless of what the circumstance. Contrary to those whom they preach at, Gandhi practiced what he taught. He used non-violence to end the injustices within South Africa, as well as in India.

Many believed that ahimsa was an act of weakness and weak, however Gandhi believed it needed enormous strength and endurance to adhere to this path, which could be followed by all. Gandhi wasn't the only person to adhere to the principles of ahimsa. However, the way he applied it was to help people and demonstrated that it was effective.

Where was he born?

Mohandas Karamchand Gandhi was born on October 2nd, 1869, in Porbandar which is a city on the coast located in Gujarat. Porbandar is a port city situated on the western coast of Kathiawar (now called

Saurashtra) in Gujarat state. Today , it is regarded for being the birthplace Mahatma who is without doubt the most influential individual India could ever produce which was recognized by the London Times.

The stunning beautiful cityscape is stunning. It also has a wealth of natural resources. It also has a harbor that conforms to international standards. Porbandar is also known for being the place of birth of Sudhama who was a religious and a poor friend to Lord Krishna.

There is a tiny memorial temple known as "Kirti Mandir" in honor of Gandhi as well as Kasturba Gandhi, his wife. Kasturba Gandhi located in the city of Porbandar.

Who were his siblings, parents, and brothers?

Karamchand Gandhi was the father of Gandhiji. The Chief Minister was Porbandar known as"the" Diwan and was married to a reverent Hindu woman known as Putlibai. Mahatma Gandhi was the couple's fourth child following the birth of two boys Laxmidas, Karsandas and daughter

Raliatbehn. His parents were part of their family of merchants of Gujarat as well as Banias through caste.

Mother of Mahatma Gandhi, Putlibai

His father was highly respected in the community in his home state. He was known as a courageous and generoushearted man. Unfortunately, he was unpopular with his temper, and was hated by the people. The first two wives of his passed away before he had children. The third one was his wife, Putlibai and eventually gave him four children.

Dad of Mahatma Gandhi, Karamchand Gandhi

Gandhi had a sister named Raliatbehn Gandhi and two brothers known as Karsandas Gandhi along with Laxmidas and Karamchand Gandhi.

What was his personality as a young person?

Mohandas was a gentle and respectful child who was a lover of playing and had fun with other children , which was normal for a child his age. Physically Mohandas was small and dark. He displayed a fearsome phobia of darkness, ghosts as well as snakes, thieves and ghosts.

Gandhi in 1876

One of the most notable characteristics of Gandhi when he was a kid is his habit of being honest. Whatever the consequences were, Gandhi would never resort to lying. He also showed immense empathy for a young boy called Okha the son of the sweeper who was considered to be lower-class and caste member according to Indian society. His childhood was a clear sign of what he was going to become in the future. When he was as a student, he wasn't not particularly bright and didn't get good marks in his tests.

Gandhi in 1883

Do you believe that he took money off from the brother he was with?

Yes. It's true that the legendary Gandhi had been into the bad company of a man named Sheikh Mehtab who was a close acquaintance of his brother. Although Gandhi knew that the man was not well-known He was nevertheless attracted by his masculine physique and strong behavior.

It was her friendship between Sheikh Mehtab which brought Gandhi to smoking cigarettes. To secure the money needed to purchase cigarettes Gandhi began to steal money and then borrowing it. Gradually the debt increased until it became increasingly difficult having to pay it back. He finally snatched the gold piece from his brother's necklace in order to pay the debt.

Gandhi together with the Sheikh Mehtab. Are you able to identify who Gandhi is in the photo?

Did he have a great education?

Gandhi was not the most brilliant student at school. However, he was a sincere committed and honest student who did not cheat even when his teacher encouraged him to cheat. In his own words Gandhiji was adamant that he would be a poor student. He was extremely timid and resisted participating in sports or additional extracurricular activity. He was said to have was unable to master multiplication tables. One of his autobiographies Gandhi writes, "My intellect must have been slow and my memory was rusty" that sheds an understanding of the struggles he faced during his school times.

Gandhi on the right side with his brother Laxmidas

Was his lady wife?

The wife of his was Karturba Gandhi born as Kastur Kapadia on the 11th of April 1869. Their wedding was organized by their families while they were both only at the age of 13.

When they got married in 1883 at the time of marriage, neither Kasturba or Mohandas were aware of the deep relationship they were about to get into. For them, marriage meant a wonderful meal with new clothing and celebrations.

Then, Kasturba joined the Indian Freedom movement with her husband. They was fighting alongside him. She passed away in his arms while they were imprisoned in Poona.

Gandhi along with wife Kasturba

Do you know if he had any children?

Yes. Mohandas as well as Kasturba Gandhi were fathers to four children called Harilal, Manilal, Ramdas and Devdas. Harilal Gandhi, their first child, was born in India in 1888. Their son Manilal was born in India four years later in 1892. The two other children of the couple had been brought up to South Africa in the year 1897 and 1900. Gandhi didn't believe in formal education, and therefore denied his children the education he received. They were angry about it during the latter years in their lives. His son, who was the elder one, was a rebel and left his family. The three younger sons took an active part in the struggle for freedom with their father.

Kasturba with her four sons

Did Gandhi have to disown his son?

Yes. Although Gandhi is acknowledged as the father of the Indian nation, unfortunately , he was not able to have a peaceful relations with his sons.

His easy-going and disciplined life style led to his children being unhappy. He faced the biggest rebellion from his daughter, Harilal Gandhi. While many adhered to the Gandhian practices, Harilal walked on the path of self-destruction that included the use of alcohol. Harilal also resisted the advice of his father, and he converted to Islam and assumed his moniker Abdullah Gandhi.

The confusion of Harilal can be seen through the manner in which he changed his mind back to Hinduism at some point later. At first, Harilal broke his ties with his family in 1911 and was later rejected from his dad. Harilal was not recognized at the funeral of his father.

What number of grandchildren did Gandhi had?

Gandhi has 13 Grandchildren from his four sons. His oldest son Harilal was blessed with four children by the marriage of his partner Chanchal. Manilal as well as his spouse Sushila were parents to three kids. Ramdas was who was married to Nirmala had two children . Devdas who was wed to Lakshmi had four children.

In the year 1976 there were 47 direct descendents from Gandhi living in various parts of the globe. Arun Gandhi, the son of Manilal is the director of origin of the "M.K. Gandhi Institute for Nonviolence" which is located in Memphis, USA. Rajmohan Gandhi is the son of Devdas is a well-known journalist political activist, social activist, and politician. Additionally, Rajmohan Gandhi is researcher in the "Center for South Asian and Middle Eastern Studies at the University of Illinois" at Urbana-Champaign, USA.

He wrote a book called "The The Good Boatman" in 1995. It was a biographie of his grandfather.

What was his subject at the university?

Gandhi took law classes at university. Gandhi was able to pass his high school examinations in 1887, at the age of 18. As per the desires of his family, who would like him to be an "Diwan" as dad, Gandhi went to England to become a barrister in 1888. Although life was not easy and it was necessary to make many changes during his time in England, Gandhi worked hard and focused to his education. He passed his bar exam without difficulty and returned to India in 1891.

Gandhi was born in London in 1890. You can decide who you consider Gandhi?

What was he doing during his time in London?

Then, in London, Gandhi studied in the "The Honourable Society" of the "Inner Temple" which is one of four most sought-after "Inns of Court" for those who wanted to study law to pursue their careers.

Gandhi was having difficulties getting used to living in London despite having Indian acquaintances who would take good care of his. He was so numb that he would cry over his mother in the late at night.

He was unable to locate vegetarian eateries inside London while spending his first days eating bread and spinach. He tried to get the appearance of Englishmen by acquiring new clothes and hairstyles. To be a part of the English society, he took dancing, music , and lessons in elocution, but he soon stopped and focused on his studies.

What was the reason Gandhi not the most successful lawyer in India?

Gandhi had studied for a long time and had a solid understanding of the law in England But Gandhi did not develop the skills how to become a competent lawyer. The shyness of his personality prevented him from making his case convincingly before a judge.

It was his first time in Bombay. He was extremely happy to win his first case. However, during the trial the judge was not able to cross-examine the witness opposing him with the utmost rigor that one would expect by lawyers. He refunded the amount clients had paid and suggested he seek the help from another lawyer.

It is possible to say that Gandhi's inability to become an attorney for civil rights was a blessing for India. His inability to practice law made him an unstoppable struggle for freedom for India which eventually brought her independence away from British Empire.

Why did he travel for a trip to South Africa?

When Gandhi returned home to India from England He was delighted to be back with his family, but unfortunately his professional career didn't go well as lawyer.

He was unable to even secure the job of being an English teacher at high school. His brother, who was a successful lawyer, gave him papers to earn some money however, Gandhi was not happy with the mundane assignments he had to perform.

He was offered a job with an important Indian company situated in South Africa. He was required to help in an ongoing case in South Africa. South African courts. It was anticipated that the work would require him to be within South Africa for a year. The company agreed to pay for all expenses while in South Africa and also pay the employee a decent pay. It was an excellent experience for Gandhi since he discovered his motivation, his philosophy, and purpose for life during his time in South Africa. When he was there the man learned a lot of things and got his mind open.

What was the reason he was removed from the first class compartment of the train?

When he was traveling to Pretoria in South Africa to Pietermaritzburg, Gandhi bought a ticket for the first class compartment. A European who was in the compartment protested against Gandhi being in it. He called railway officials who advised Gandhi that whites and people of working class weren't allowed access to first-class compartments. They demanded that he get out of the coach , but Gandhi did not agree and showed his ticket. After warning Gandhi the officials, they were forcefully thrown on the platform along with his baggage. This was a pivotal moment within the history of Gandhi and the world, as this is the time Gandhi was aware of his discrimination based on color and decided to combat it.

What was his job when he was in South Africa?

Gandhi began his career working for "Dada Abdulla and Co." on their long-running case before the court in South Africa and also worked as a legal representative of"Muslim Indian Traders" "Muslim Indian Traders". He was scheduled to be there for a year however he extended his stay to 21 years.

Gandhi participating at protests taking place in South Africa

While was in South Africa, Gandhi was shocked by the discrimination exhibited to people of all races, including Indians. Gandhi was aware of the brutality of the government against the citizens who resided in South Africa. This is the place where Gandhi began to fight social injustices by writing letters to newspapers and his lectures. He also participated in debates and filed numerous petitions. The timid man who struggled to make a statement in court returned to South Africa as a fearless leader who was able to influence people with his speeches.

A policeman confronting Gandhi in South Africa

What was it he was fighting for?

Gandhi was a champion for human rights for Indians throughout South Africa. He began by establishing"the "Natal Indian Congress" in 1894, which was a way to make the entire population of Indians of South Africa a single political group.

It is the Natal Indian Congress

He encouraged peaceful protests among his supporters. He employed this method to defend rights of the human race. He demanded that the government eliminate taxes imposed on Indian workers, and to grant them the right to vote. He was determined to improve the standard of living of the people of color living in South Africa.

He began to protest using the "satyagraha" and was forced to spend two months in prison after being sparked by a gang. He was able to secure some legal rights granted to citizens.

When did he return to India?

Gandhi was a man who left Bombay as an attorney who was unable to make his case to the court for two decades - came back two years later on January 9 1915 as a hero, who stood against injustice in society.

He was averse to the political scene and other social activity until he was able to be able to study and comprehend the circumstances in India. He was heavily in the direction that were taught by Gopal Krishna Gokhale. Following the massacre at Amritsar on the night of 1919 Gandhi was a satyagraha protester and launched his massive protest for the liberation of India from British rule.

He chose to wear Indian clothes upon the return trip to India

What was the reason Gandhi design the clothes he wore?

The cottage industry of cotton was totally destroyed and as it was the cause Indian craftsmen became extremely poor. The cotton produced in India was shipped to the cotton mills in Manchester in England which was where clothes were produced and then sold in the market. This led to the job loss and financial hardship among those who relied on clothing. Gandhi consequently did not wear clothing made by the British to protest. He urged his followers to create their own clothes and reject imports from England that brought hardship in the villages in India.

What was his reason for opposing British rule?

Gandhi stood up against the British by non-violent, passive resistance. His weapons were not swords, sticks or guns, but the love, discipline and truth. Satyagraha is the Sanskrit word that means "insistence on the truth" This is the word Gandhi employed to fight the evils in British Empire. British Empire.

In the protest marches, police brutally beat him and his supporters brutally, however Gandhi did not stand up for himself. He continued to march regardless of the hardships the cost. His tactics made the British feel guilty because their consciences were affected by his actions.

Gandhi in an anti-protest march

What was the purpose of Non-Cooperation Movement?

"The "Non-Cooperation movement" was one of the three crucial milestones in India's struggle for freedom. Gandhi was a co-operative partner in a joint effort with British throughout World War 1, but things changed drastically after the introduction of the Rowlatt Act, Jallianwallah Bagh massacre, and The Khilafat issue.

It is the Jallianwalla Bagh site was built a few months after the murder in 1919 by Brigadier General Reginald Dyer

Gandhi was unhappy by the British Government, so he started his own "Non-Cooperation movement" to India. The goal was to use non-violence, non-cooperation, and peacefully fight in opposition to and against the British Raj. When the Indians removed their support from the British government It became increasingly hard to the British to control the administration in India.

Gandhi along with Lord as well as Lady Mountbatten

The non-cooperation movement was officially started in August 1920. Gandhi returned the awards that he received for his military service in the hands of the British Government. The purpose that the group was pursuing was to achieve justice for those who were killed by the terrorists in Jallianwala Bagh, change of marriage law and the Khilafat issue and finally to achieve Swaraj, i.e. self-rule for India.

What exactly is the purpose of Salt March?

"The "salt march" was also referred to as salt satyagraha was an unarmed march that was that was organized by Gandhi and his followers to protest the unjust "salt tax" which was imposed by British upon Indians.

Indians were not allowed to by British to make or sell salt, thus monopolizing the essential ingredient in cooking. Many poor

Indians were unable to afford salt that was extremely expensive.

Prior to the start of this protest Gandhi was personally informing and appealing to Gandhi to British viceroy to change the tax on salt, however it was not accepted. On the 12th March of 1930 Gandhi and 78 followers set off on a 240-mile, 23-day journey that began in Sabarmati Ashram to end on Dandi beach. Gandhi would challenge the British and create salt in Dandi beach.

Was he doing to the people who were not able to be touched in India?

Unfortunately, Indian society was divided according to social class and caste boundaries. Many preferred to refer to themselves as upper castes while looking at people of lower social class and considered them lower castes as well as untouchables. Gandhi was born in Bania, the highest Bania caste, and showed empathy for the untouchables as a young child.

He often played and treat Okha the son of the sweeper as a child. To combat the enduring evils that arose throughout India, Gandhi went on a hunger strike in September 1932 to protest against the discrimination against people who were not considered to be a part of the society. Indians protested by releasing several public spaces and temples dedicated to people who were not touched for their first-ever time Indian history.

He was the one who inspired him to create his group "Harijan Sevak Sangh" to fight for the rights of the people who were thought to be untouchables. He referred to them as Harijan which means "children from God". He worked tirelessly to improve the conditions of those who were not touched.

Gandhi with an leper

What was the purpose of Quit India Movement?

Quit India Movement or "Bharat Chhodo Andolan" was launched by Gandhi in

August 1942, requesting an orderly departure of the British of India. On the 8th of August in 1942 the AICC (All India Congress Committee) began a massive non-violent protest to demand an end to British rule over India. Gandhi created a motto "karo maaro" which means 'do or die and enticed all Indian in the country to defend freedom for their country.

Gandhi along with Nehru in 1942

The British responded with a harsh stance to the movement, detaining leaders and resorting in a brutal beatings of protesters who were not armed. They also fired on the protesters. They also restricted the rights of civil liberties, freedom of speech, and freedom of the press . They also were arrested many Indian leaders. After the arrest of several leaders, the crowd became violent, which led to violence.

Even though there was a resounding defeat of the Quit India effort was thwarted however, the British eventually agreed to end their involvement in India but only after World War 2 had ended.

When did India become independent?

After a lot of struggles, sacrifices, and protests by Indian liberation fighters India was declared independent on August 15th, 1947. The moment of victory was also accompanied with sadness for Gandhi because of the division of the nation that resulted in ethnic protests.

Although he strongly disproved the idea of a division between India However, the British didn't pay much attention to his work. Instead of celebrating the independence that was India, Gandhi spent the days following Independence days in a state of fasting until death to ensure peace and harmony for his country.

Based on the work of scholar Jens Arup Seip lots of bloodshed was avoided during the partition because of an effort by Gandhi and his supporters.

What was Jinnah and did he have a friend in Gandhi?

Mohammed Ali Jinnah, a politician and lawyer is regarded as the first president of Pakistan. While they were both associates, Gandhi and Jinnah were not close friendships. While Gandhi was known to Jinnah as "Brother Jinnah" and they were both arch adversaries and their ideologies were totally different.

Even though they had their disagreements however, they had a respect for one another. Gandhi believed Jinnah as a courageous and unquestionably honest, whereas Jinnah, for his part Jinnah believed Gandhi as one of the best men of all time.

There was a disagreement over a variety of aspects, including their split in India. Jinnah was adamantly opposed to the Khilafat campaign of Gandhi because he believed that it was an acceptance of religious fanaticism. Jinnah also deplored as a "satyagraha movements".

Why was he fasting all time?

Gandhi lived a straightforward and disciplined existence and his diet was comprised of a light vegetarian diet. He began his fasts to cleanse himself and as a way of protest against the status quo later. The fasts became an instrument to help him to follow the path of non-violence. It was also considered to be a type of spiritual action for Gandhi.

As he became a part of the India's independence movement, the he decided to fast 17 times, with the longest of which lasted for 21 days. Although fasting is an easy method but not everyone can follow this route without a reason or motivation behind it is the inside of oneself.

Gandhi eating his last meal prior to beginning of his fast in 1939.

What exactly is Satyagraha?

"Satya" is a word that means truth,"Satya" means truth "agraha" refers to insistence. Therefore, the literal meaning of satyagraha is insisting or imposing truth or the force of truth, and the power generated by adherence to the truth. It's a peaceful method of protesting against injusticeand being compassionate and loving to human beings.

Gandhi did not attempt to destroy or even break his adversaries, he set out to transform their hearts with his methods. He believed that by his peaceful methods with love and compassion it would be possible to nudge those who oppressed them off of their evil practices. It was believed that the Civil Disobedience and Non-Cooperation Movement were founded on the premise of Satyagraha.

What was the number of times he had to have to go to the jail?

Gandhi was jailed 6 occasions during his time in South Africa for opposing apartheid. The British were able to arrest and detain him around 7 times in India for peaceful protests against the colonial system.

The arrests he was made in India ran for three decades beginning on April 10, 1919 10th March 1922 5th May 1930 4th January 1932 1st August 1933, and concluding with his final detention on the 9th of August in 1942.

The British faced a difficult time in keeping Gandhi in jail since there was war in the air to overthrow the dictatorship Adolf Hitler. Gandhi frequently participated in a hunger strikes in prison, which was a nightmare for the British. The death of Gandhi in jail would not only cause the mobs to revolt in India however, it would also cause them to lose their credibility around the world.

When did he die and how?

Gandhi was a warrior in ahimsa, peace, and peace throughout the course of his life He was the subject of brutal attack of

Nathuram Godse, who shot Gandhi at point blank range using an Beretta pistol on the 30th of January 1948.

Gandhi was in the process of addressing an assembly of prayer in Gandhi Smriti (back when it was known as Birla House) with his nieces when an assassins targeted the man. When the three bullets landed inside the chest of his victim, Gandhi collapsed with the word "Hey Ram" in his mouth.

Godse was Godse, a Hindu nationalist, and his conspirators disdain Gandhi since they believed that they supported Pakistan. Godse did not support the principle of non-violence and was also a pacifist. He was mourned, not just in India however, but throughout the world.

How can I show reverence to the Mahatma?

After his assassination Gandhi was buried in the Western Bank of Yamuna. Because he was one of the most adored national leaders his remains were scattered across the oceans and in all important rivers in India.

You can pay homage to the Mahatma Gandhi by visiting his memorial in Raj Ghat, which is close to the National Gandhi Museum in New Delhi. It is also the location in which Gandhiji was cremated.

It is the Raj Ghat in Delhi. Location: Gandhi Smriti, Raj Ghat, New Delhi, India

Visitors must remove their shoes before they enter the memorial to show a token of respect for the most powerful leader India has ever had. The memorial is made of black marble and has it's words "Hey Ram" (the Mahatma's final words) written on the stone.

The memorial site is surrounded by an endless flame that burns at one end. It is also surrounded by gorgeous lawn and a wall which stops the flow of the River Yamuna. People from across the globe go to Raj Ghat to pay respect to the Mahatma.

It is also possible to honor Mahatma by practicing ahimsa, which means non-violence towards any living thing, never stealing from anyone Never lying, and always being respectful of all people. He once said "You should become the change you would like to be able to see around the world".

www.ingramcontent.com/pod-product-compliance
Lightning Source LLC
Chambersburg PA
CBHW050405120526
44590CB00015B/1841